A Parent's Love

By

Mark H Stahl

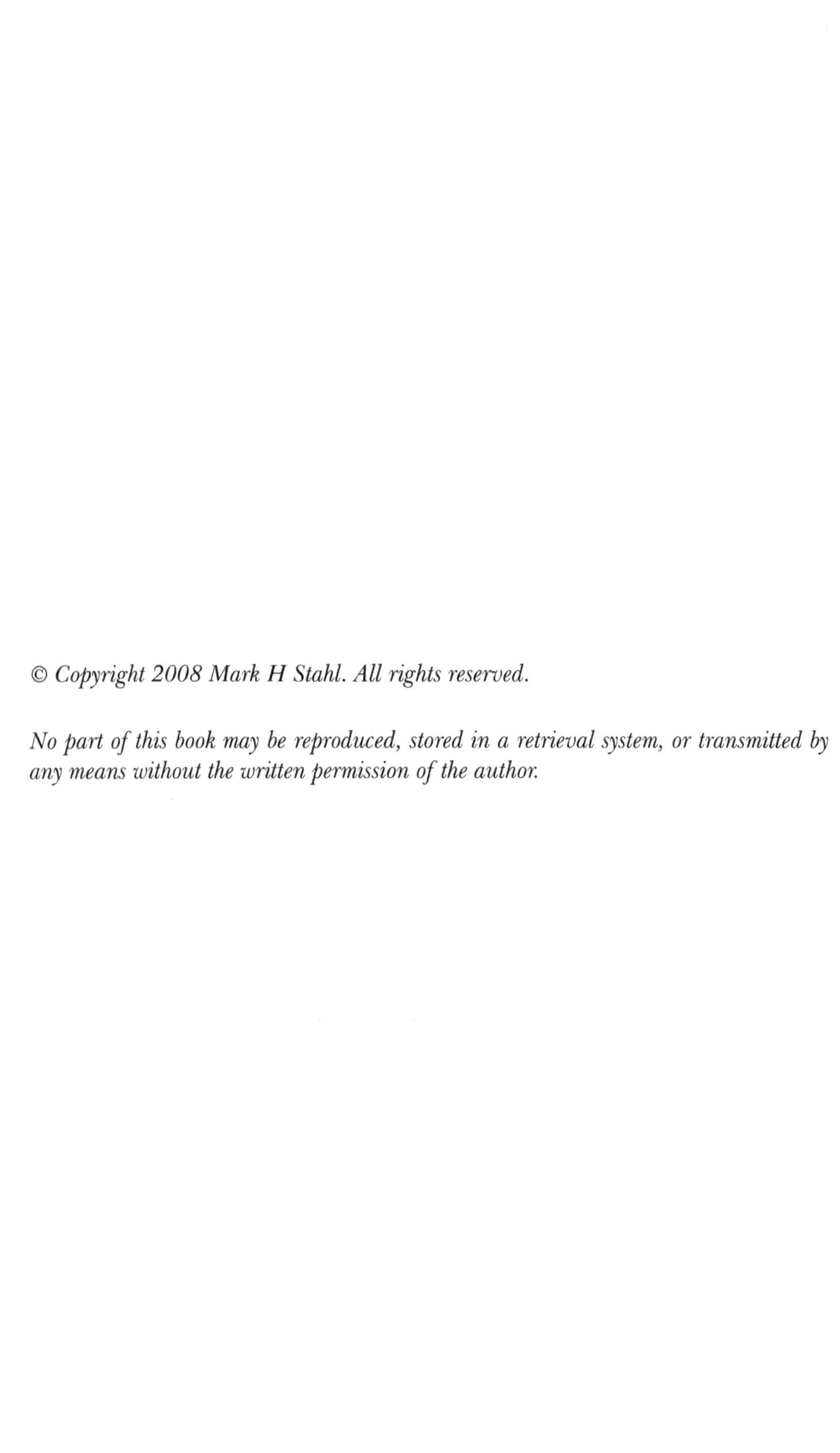

CONTENTS

CHAPTER 1

It was on August 30th, 2000 just around midnight I received a phone call that changed my life forever. My son Todd had been in an accident and was being life lined to the hospital.

It was a Wednesday and I had just gone to bed an hour earlier when I received a call from Belinda, my son's mother. She said, "Todd has been in an accident, and they're taking him by helicopter from Johnson County to Methodist Hospital." I arranged to meet Belinda at the hospital's emergency room as soon as possible. My wife, Linda, and I hurriedly threw on some clean clothes and headed to Methodist, located near downtown Indianapolis. We lived on the southeast side of town and it took us about twenty minutes to get to the hospital's emergency room parking lot.

Belinda greeted us as we entered through the hospital doors. She had arrived at Methodist just as the helicopter carrying Todd was landing on the hospital's roof. I must confess, from that moment on, my memory of time is nothing but a blur. Minutes became hours and hours could have been just minutes. For that reason my reference to times in this story are only benchmarks, rather than a specific time period.

Belinda had already checked in with the emergency waiting room attendant who sat at a counter type desk quietly reading behind a glass-enclosed room. While we waited for word from the hospital staff, Belinda explained what had transpired that evening.

Just a few minutes before Belinda called Linda and me at home, she had received a call from a lady with a cell phone. The lady explained that she was traveling with her young daughter down a remote country road. When she started around a curve in the road she saw a vehicle down a small embankment with its lights still on. She pulled her car over to the side of the road to get a closer look and saw that the car was heavily damaged. She then got out of her car to check if there was someone injured inside the car.

The young mother told Belinda that the car must have hit a tree with great force and bounced away from it. The driver's side door was open and she saw no one in the car. As she rounded the front of the vehicle she found Todd lying along the roadside a few feet away from his wrecked compact car. The only scenario she could figure out was that Todd must had enough strength left to drag himself out of the car and up the small embankment. After using her cell phone to call 911, the lady tried to comfort Todd until emergency crews could arrive. The Good Samaritan asked Todd if there was anyone she could contact. At that point, Todd was just conscious enough to give her his home phone number, or at least what he thought to be his home phone number. According to the young lady, Todd had told her that he wasn't' sure. It was either his home phone number or Pizza Huts. After what seemed to her to be a very long period of time an ambulance arrived at the scene. Paramedics leaped out of the ambulance and started to attend to Todd's injuries. They cautiously placed Todd on a gurney and loaded him into the back of the ambulance. The paramedics told the woman that they would be transporting him to the county hospital.

The kind lady who had stopped to assist Todd then called the number that Todd had given her. Concerned she told Belinda that Todd's accident looked very serious and he was being taken to Johnson County Memorial Hospital.

Belinda learned in a subsequent phone call to hospital, that Todd injuries were far worse than they were capable of treating. The attendant explained that they were going to Lifeline him to Methodist Hospital. He explained to Belinda that Todd had suffered head trauma and Methodist was far better equipped to deal with the type of injuries he had sustained.

Linda, Belinda, and I waited a half-hour until the two large automated doors swung out from the inner section of the emergency room. The night shift nurse walked briskly through the doors and directly to us. This was probably an unusual night at Methodist, which was one of the larger hospitals in the state; besides the three of us, there were relatively very few people in the waiting room. The nurse who had approached us started to explain that they were cleaning Todd up, taking x-rays, and a doctor would be examining him soon.

We waited a short while later, and then a doctor appeared through the same doors that the nurse had previously entered. He explained that Todd had sustained severe head trauma and he was in critical condition. He said, "A neurologist on call that evening had been summoned to further evaluate his condition." Belinda and I were then allowed to go to the bedside of our son. We followed the doctor around the maze of corridors in the emergency room, an area of the hospital I was already familiar with. Just a couple of years previously I had accompanied a friend of mine, a Muscular Dystrophy patient, to that very same hospital's emergency room.

The doctor stopped Belinda and I just outside Todd's room. He told us to wait momentarily while he checked to see if it was okay for us to enter. The doctor reappeared from the room and pulled back the curtain. I was in complete shock when I first glanced in the room before me. I firmly believe nothing could have prepared me for the scene that would lie before me.

On the floor scattered throughout the room laid blood soaked towels. In the middle of the room Todd was lying with his eyes closed on a hospital gurney bed. The sheets on the bed and those covering him were spotted with blood and his face was covered with scratches and large scrapes. The first signs of blue rings were beginning to appear around both of his eyes. Straps had been placed around Todd's wrists, because of his serious head injuries; the staff wanted to limit his movement. Todd appeared to be sleeping, but his head suddenly sprung up and he began to scream wanting to be released. An attendant would gently encourage him to lie his head back down, and Todd's eyes would close and he would again appear to be unconscious.

Belinda took position on one side of Todd's bed while I stationed myself on the other. The doctor stood at the foot of the bed and began to tell us what they had found thus far. He said, "Todd must have hit his head extremely hard against the steering wheel of his car. It appears his skull had been fractured at eye level with the fracture running towards the back of the head." The doctor's primary concern was the amount of damage the brain had sustained resulting from the force of the impact. While he was unsure whether other injuries had also been incurred, he couldn't do any further examinations until a neurologist had evaluated Todd's condition.

It wasn't long before the on call neurologist had arrived. He had examined the x-rays taken earlier that evening but requested yet another set be made right away. Belinda and I returned to the waiting room where we rejoined Linda, and waited for the results of that second set of x-rays. I briefly explained to Linda what had transpired in the emergency room. She grabbed my hand to comfort me as the tears started to well up in my eyes while I told her about the condition of the room when we first entered it.

After what seemed to be an eternity the neurologist came out to speak with us. The three of us followed him back to a room where the set of x-rays was hanging on a lighted cabinet. The doctor pointed out two gray areas on the x-rays, one towards the front of Todd's brain and one in the back near the base. He didn't "pull any punches" as he explained that Todd was in very critical condition. His brain had definitely been bruised from the impact of the collision. His main concern at this point was the possibility of the brain swelling, thereby causing pressure within the skull. To lower the activity of the brain and aid in the healing process, Todd would be treated with drugs while being kept in a conscious state. The doctor told us that they could only keep him in a conscious state as long as Todd didn't thrash about too much causing greater damage to the brain.

The doctor went on to explain that he preferred to keep Todd conscious, but if that failed, Todd would have to be place into a drug-induced semi-comatose state and finally a full comatose state if nothing else worked. He told us that Todd's chances of recovery would be far greater if they could control the swelling of the brain before they got to that point.

Belinda, Linda, and I were then allowed back to the area of the emergency room where Todd was being treated. The hospital staff had cleaned up the blood soaked towels on the floor and the sheets covering Todd had been changed to nice clean ones.

Two men dressed in green hospital scrubs entered the room and told us Todd was being transferred to the Head Trauma Critical Care Unit on the fifth floor of the hospital. Belinda, Linda and I were allowed to ride the elevator with Todd and were then escorted to the waiting room of the fifth floor unit.

I can't tell you what time it was when we walked into that waiting area. I know it was a lot later than I expected, maybe close to 5:00 AM. Two men in disheveled clothing were soundly asleep on plastic-cushioned sofas; each appearing to be in very uncomfortable positions. Later I could testify that they were.

I don't know about Belinda, but Linda and I had slept maybe an hour or two before Belinda's phone call. None the less we weren't the least bit tired. We quietly slipped to one side of the waiting room and whispered so as not to disturb the two sleeping gentlemen. I was full of questions for Belinda --- "What was Todd doing on that road? Had he been drinking?" Of course, Belinda didn't have all the answers, but what she did know was that Todd had earlier that evening gone to visit a friend. Upon his arrival, he had called Belinda to let her know that he was there. As to the drinking question, we later found out that a blood alcohol test completed at the hospital indicated a level that exceeded the legal limit. We never inquired how high that level was.

During the remainder of the morning hours we acquainted ourselves with the Critical Care Unit's policies and procedures. The waiting room was open 24 hours day and one-hour patient visitations were allowed at 9:00 AM, 2:00 PM and 7:00 PM. The room was equipped with several pieces of furniture, four pay telephones and free coffee and tea. At around 6:00 AM one of the nurses informed us that Todd had been settled into his room and we could go see him. As she escorted us through a couple of sliding glass doors and down the corridors, I noticed that all the rooms in the unit were only three sided with a curtain that could be stretched across the front. Most of the curtains were open, and only a few of the rooms were occupied. At the end of the hall was Todd's room. By this time he had been cleaned up and looked as if he were sleeping. Wires and tubes were attached to his arms and fingers, and numerous monitors stood beside and above his bed outputting data that meant nothing to me at the time but with which I would become well acquainted.

Todd would thrash about occasionally, moan incoherently and then settle back down again. The nurse informed us that he was still trying at times to get up --- an action that worried them considerably since his movements and jostling could cause greater damage to the brain. While Belinda stood by Todd's bed clutching his hand and patting it gently, I stood on the other side of the bed watching his chest heave with heavy breathing. Suddenly, Todd tried once again to sit up so I placed my hand on his chest and told him to lie back down. A few minutes later a member of the nursing staff asked that we leave so they could go through their routine to check Todd's vitals.

Having gone back to the waiting room, we started the process of calling our families and work. I just made two phone calls myself, my sister Clare a public grade school teacher and the office of my boss.

I knew there would be no one at work at this hour in the morning so I left a message on the recorder that I wouldn't be in that day, because of my son's accident. My sister Clare was getting ready to go to school and volunteered to skip it and come to the hospital. I told her right now there wasn't anything to do but wait and she should go on to work. I did ask her to call my dad, brother and other sister. She said she would and told me she'd be there as soon as school let out.

I would have called my other brother and sister myself, but I didn't want to have to go and locate more change for the pay phone. I will admit that I would have had a hard time telling Dad of Todd's situation without breaking down in tears.

Our family had gone through a lot this past month, with just having to place mom in a nursing home. Mom's dementia had progressed to the point where dad couldn't take care of her at home any more. Dad was a few months away from being 84 years old. Mom had shown the first signs of Alzheimer's disease around five years ago and Dad did everything he could to keep Mom comfortably at home.

The first year or two of the disease was hard to pick up on. Mom would forget little things and dad would get upset with her. My sister Clare and I were the first to pick up on mom's condition when she started to repeat the stories she had told us just fifteen minutes earlier. Finally my older sister too had commented on mom constantly repeating herself. Dad was the last to acknowledge mom's condition. He was in constant denial and would just say things like she's always been that way. It wasn't until Mom turned to him one day and asked him what were the names of their children that dad finally decided to take her to the doctor's office.

Over the period of a few months the doctor would ask mom simple questions. Such as who was the president of United States, what day or month was it, and of course names of family members. Mom would stumble around and try to answer the questions and Dad would defend her saying he probably couldn't answer some of the doctor's questions.

As time progressed so did the disease. Mom would make up stories and started to call dad, "the guy who was living in her house." Supposedly, he needed a place to live and she was helping him out. Soon she lost the ability to communicate and started to wander. Dad was very careful about keeping an eye on her, but one time when exhausted from being mom's caregiver he fell asleep in his chair. It wasn't ten minutes later he woke and discovered Mom missing.

He frantically searched the neighborhood and finally after about a half-hour decided to call the Beech Grove police. Fortunately, they had already found a very confused lady about a mile and a half from the house. Even then dad didn't want to let her go. He installed high locks on the doors and requested a medic alert medallion from the Alzheimer's association. It wasn't until Dad's legs started giving out he felt he couldn't provide for her care anymore.

Dad really felt guilty about having to place her in a special memory care unit and it took a lot of reassuring from his kids to convince him he was doing the right thing. It was pretty hard on all of the kids to watch mom's mental health decline. She had gone from the mother we loved to a child over a long period of time. The deterioration was so gradual that it became harder for us to remember her the way she was before the disease took its toll. As hard as it was on us kids, I can't imagine the pain my father was experiencing. He had to let go of the woman he had married and loved for over fifty years.

CHAPTER 2

Linda took the elevator down to the hospital's cafeteria and brought back some rolls for all of us. Linda and I sat together on one side of the large waiting room and said very little. Belinda was still on the phone trying to reach family and friends. As I sat there, I looked at Belinda and found it hard to believe that we had been married for ten years. In reality we were married for ten years only on paper --- the last four years were more like two people simply living together in the same house.

I can remember meeting her for the first time at her home on the far south side of Indianapolis. My best friend, Leo, was someone with whom I had worked with at St. Francis Hospital in Beech Grove, a suburb of the City of Indianapolis. I became very close to his family and one of his cousins, Ron, who was also a good friend with whom I had gone to grade school. On Memorial Day each year their extended family would gather at Belinda's parent's home and have an "Indianapolis 500" race day picnic. They were kind enough to invite me one year, and I'll never forget the fun I had at that picnic and at the picnics that would follow in subsequent years.

Badminton, volleyball, cards, horseshoes, and basketball were played regularly. A radio broadcast of the race was aired, and the best part of the day was the pitch-in luncheon. Every year someone would bring a new dish to be sampled --- if it was good, they were required to bring it every year thereafter. It was time spent with some of the nicest people you could ever meet. I don't know if it was Leo who introduced me to Belinda --- it could have been anyone. I do recall that as we engaged in conversation that day, she seemed to be someone with whom you could easily converse. It was probably a week later that I asked her out to a movie. We dated a couple of years and were then married.

Before I continue with this story, I should give you a little of my own background. I was born in the early fifties to a very middle-class family. My father was a blue-collar worker --- my mother was a stay-at-home mom who had dinner on the table promptly at five o'clock every evening. I have one older and one younger sister and a younger brother.

Dad took us kids to church every Sunday while Mom always managed to be sick on Sunday morning, recovering nicely right after services were over. My father was of third generation German descent. Mom was the daughter of Italian immigrants and the first of her family to be born in America. All of us, including Mom and Dad, were educated in the Catholic school system. Dad was the disciplinarian in the family, and my mother was the "wait until your father gets home" type of mom. That was good for us kids, since we had to do something extremely bad for Mom to really report us. Although she would threaten us, she was usually afraid to tell dad later. I don't know if she was afraid of Dad spanking us or of him yelling at her for not handling the situation herself.

Belinda and I were married in nineteen seventy-three. Her family and I became very close, mainly because they treated me as one of their own. Since my greatest aspiration at that time was to be a writer and a family man I felt this was the perfect fit for me.

I had bought a small two-bedroom home prior to getting married and the first addition to our family was a dog named Jessie. We were driving down one of the neighborhood streets and Belinda suddenly yelled, "stop." I pulled the car over and we went back to a house where there was a sign that said free puppies. In a small cage in front were four small dogs. Belinda picked out the one with three black paws and one white one. Though Belinda picked Jessie out, she soon became my responsibility to look after and I don't think she'd argue the fact that Jessie became my dog.

We only stayed at the small house for one year and we purchased a new one from a builder on the Southeast side of town. It was a three-bedroom tri-level with a two-car garage and a basement. Every Friday and Saturday night we would have friends over and would play some kind of card or board game. I was sitting on top of the world back then. I had everything I could imagine --- a wife, tons of good family and friends, a home, a dog named Jessie, and the hope of having a child. These were my "picket fence" dreams all coming true.

Belinda and I waited a couple of years before we decided to have children. We had discussed it while we were engaged, but Belinda had a job that she really loved and I wasn't going to force the issue until she was ready. Belinda finally approached me on her own and I couldn't have been happier.

We tried for about a year and we began to worry that something was wrong. We both made appointments with our respective doctors. My doctor ordered a sperm test for me, and the results came back a week later. The doctor told me my sperm count was low and it was highly unlikely I would ever be able to have children of my own. At first I couldn't believe what the doctor had told me and questioned if the test could have been wrong. The doctor said that was unlikely, but I was welcome to get a second opinion.

I was devastated by the news the doctor gave me that day. I remember having to tell Belinda that evening and just breaking down in tears. At that point it seemed all my dreams were shattered.

Later that same evening, Belinda and I discussed the possibility of adoption. We both knew a family with adopted children and we decided it probably was our best, and perhaps, our only option.

There was a Catholic home for unwed mothers just outside of Beech Grove and only a few miles from where we lived. Belinda and I both thought it was the first place we should call to get more information. We set an appointment with a counselor at the facility and were given some basic information.

In the initial meeting we were informed of how much money would be required and I believe it was close to $2500.00. That fee was mainly what the agency charged which included the cost for the testing, counseling, and evaluating. It didn't include the cost of an attorney to finalize the adoption in the courts, which would cost another $500.00.

Three thousand dollars was a lot of money back then to a couple just starting out, but we didn't give it a second thought and made an application right away. We were told we could choose to specify a boy or girl, or take first available either sex. I'll admit I was leaning towards wanting a boy, but we decided that either would be a welcome addition to our family and our home.

We were told the adoption process was long and tedious. Belinda and I underwent extensive psychiatric testing, physical examinations, and at least three home studies where a counselor would come out to our home, interview, and evaluate us. Two and one-half years after we initially made application, I became the father of a ten-day-old baby boy on June 5, 1979.

CHAPTER 3

Belinda's sister, Joyce, and her daughter arrived at the hospital around 8:00 a.m. that morning. I hadn't seen Joyce for a few years, but she still looked the same. Her daughter though was a different story. I hadn't seen her since our divorce. She was probably three years older than Todd and she into a nice young lady.

After greeting them, I excused myself so Belinda could fill them in on Todd's condition. Shortly thereafter a nurse entered the waiting room. She informed us that Todd's condition had not improved --- he was still very critical and had to be stabilized. Todd was still trying to get up now and then and they were worried that he could inflict more damage to his brain. Therefore, the doctor had decided to induce him into a semi-comatose state. I remembered the staff telling us earlier that placing him in the different states of consciousness would not be to Todd's advantage. For some reason though it seemed to be a logical choice to me so it didn't concern me as much as expected.

Throughout the day various people came by or called to check on Todd's condition. My sister, Clare, spent much of the afternoon with me, and other family members called and asked if they should come by. I just didn't see the point at that time. It was purely a waiting game to see if the swelling of the brain could be controlled. To be honest, I was full of anxiety and I didn't want to deal with a lot of people coming in asking about Todd's condition. I was trying to maintain a positive attitude and maintain a brave presence about myself.

Early in the afternoon, Chaplain Steel from the Police Department stopped by and offered his assistance. I told him to please keep Todd in his prayers and that's all that anyone can do at this point.

Later that afternoon while visiting Todd, I tried to familiarize myself with the various monitors being used for his care in order to get a better grasp of his situation. One of the nurses explained some of the more critical readings, one of which was the measurement of the pressure of the brain against the skull. It was extremely important to keep the pressure down below the digital read out of twenty. At that time, the numbers were floating between ten or twelve. Earlier they had been fluctuating between sixteen and eighteen. The nurse explained that they were trying to control further swelling of the brain with the use of various drugs.

I don't remember exactly how the drugs controlled the brain from swelling. It could have directly affected the brain's swelling or just calmed down the activity causing less trauma allowing the brain time to heal itself. They had just administered another dosage of the drug a few minutes earlier, which accounted for the lower reading Todd had at this time. Right now the doctors were just waiting to see if they could control the swelling enough to stabilize Todd's condition.

That night I went back once again at regular visiting hours and checked on Todd. I was surprised by how busy the floor was at that time of night with various people coming and going. Back in the waiting room, family members of other patients would come by and talk. We heard many stories of the circumstances behind their loved ones ending up in a critical care unit. Some were due to accidents, others to disease. One of the men in the ward had a peculiar type of cancer and had three family members visiting. I spoke to the man's son and he told me the cancer had riddled his father's body. He has been moved around to various areas of the hospital, which specialized in different fields of medicine. The family knew this was his last stop and that he would not be leaving this floor alive.

Two of the accident victims were young teenage boys from separate incidents clowning around on motorized three wheelers. Neither of the victims wore a helmet at the time and both had suffered severe head trauma injuries. I'm not the one to preach, but there seems to be a lesson there somewhere.

I watched the people come and go from the waiting room and I wondered if it was this busy every night. I had been in several hospital waiting rooms over the years, including emergency rooms, but this critical care unit had a different feel to it. I guess it could have been just me, but it seemed the anxiety level was higher here.

I'm the kind of person that looks at the whole picture. I thought how this is just one waiting room of thousands around the world filled with worried people waiting and hoping for the recovery of their loved ones. I bowed my head and prayed not just for Todd, but all of those injured patients, their friends and family members all going through difficult times.

Belinda, Linda and I did not want to leave the hospital that night, so we camped out in the visitors' waiting room. One gentleman had staked claim to one of two small sofas in the room, so Belinda found a recliner, Linda took the other sofa, and I pulled two chairs together. While the receptionist had earlier explained that there were facilities nearby where we could stay for a small fee, we did not even consider it an option. Not because of the expense, although minimal, but because we just wanted to be close to Todd.

The nurse attending Todd that night was kind enough to see that we had pillows and blankets. I remember feeling exhausted. I also remember taking forever to get comfortable in those chairs. Linda and Belinda didn't fair any better, for they both complained of aching backs in the morning. If the hospital's intention was to equip the waiting room with uncomfortable furniture to discourage people like us I'm sure it worked for some people.

As I attempted to get some sleep that night, I thought back to the day Belinda and I went to St. Elizabeth's Home to pick up our new baby boy who had been born May 26, 1979.

Without breaking any confidentiality rules, we were given as much information as possible about Todd's parent's background. I have to admit, however, that I wasn't paying much attention to what was being said --- I was just beaming and so excited to get home with my son. Fortunately, we were given all that information in written form as well.

Todd's natural mother was nineteen years old. She was 5'5" tall and weighed over two hundred pounds. His father was 6'3" and was in the military. Included in the information was a complete medical history of the mother's family. All similar information for the father was listed as "unknown". I remember commenting to Belinda that I wondered if the father even knew about Todd.

Before we even left the adoption agency that day, Todd had relieved himself all over Belinda as she tried to change him. While I laughed, Belinda commented that she didn't mind a bit. She, too, was so excited with our new son and couldn't wait to get him home. We had been preparing for this day for almost three years and it had finally arrived.

The day after we brought Todd home the house was filled with friends and relatives who came by to see the baby. Each of them brought a gift of some kind, many of which were football related since that was my favorite sport. Some of the gifts bore the logo of my favorite team, the Chicago Bears, of course that was before the Colts came to Indianapolis.

A year before Todd's arrival, Belinda and I sustained considerable damage to our home when a tornado hit our neighborhood. The roof and attached garage were completely blown away, and the rain that followed the wind soaked the drywall and insulation beyond salvaging. The rain destroyed all of our furniture, record albums, books, and a lot of personal items we had acquired throughout the years.

I can remember the night of the storm like it was yesterday. It was a Saturday night in June and we were all gathered at my brother's house about three miles from our housing addition. My brother, Michael and his wife Liz had called earlier in the week and said "you're always having everyone over to your house why don't you all come over to ours this weekend for a cook out." They had also invited Belinda's cousins Leo and Rick (Ron's brother), who were like brothers to me by now and we all accepted knowing that Liz was one of the best cooks in town.

Michael and Liz were living in a small addition and their back yard bordered a city golf course. We were sitting on the patio and we noticed it getting dark to the West. The forecast had called for evening thunderstorms, but we thought it was suppose to hit later that night. As the skies darkened we knew it was time to head in doors.

I don't believe I've ever seen a storm move in so fast in all my life. We looked out the patio doors and saw it approach across the golf course. The rain came down in sheets and the wind howled against the house. I remember the patio table we had just ate at rising off the ground almost floating and setting back down again.

I can't tell you how long the storm lasted, but it seemed like quite some time. When the initial thrust of it was over we all sat down to play some cards. It was about a half-hour later the phone rang and it was my older sister Jackie asking if I was there.

Jackie lived a couple blocks away from Belinda and I in the same addition. She said, "I better get home." I asked, "What for?" She then said, "You may not have a home." Belinda and I jumped into our Volkswagen Beetle and headed home. We got only a mile from Michael's house and couldn't get any farther. We were driving down Beech Grove's Main Street and just after Thirteenth Ave a large tree had fallen across the road. Thirteenth was completely underwater from water rushing down the street heading to the creek not a hundred feet away.

I was afraid to take the low riding VW through the water so I turned around and headed back to Michael's house. Leo had a Ford Econoline van and volunteered to take us home in it. Rick came along too and we set off once again.

We soon got to the spot where Belinda and I had to turn around earlier and Leo's van went through the water with no problem. Just as we crossed over the bridge another tree limb blocked our way and we had to go around the block back to Main Street just past where the trees had fallen.

Heading east on Main we passed the small town stores that lined both sides of the street. Most of the stores on both sides of the street had been shattered and broke glass littered the sidewalks.

Just outside the town of Beech Grove First Avenue turns into Emerson Ave and we proceeded to go south on it to Thompson Road. We turned left on Thompson and headed east to the entrance to our addition. After we had turned onto First Avenue and all the way to where we were now there was very little evidence of the storm we saw that hit Main Street in Beech Grove.

As we headed further back to the north into the addition we started again to see some broken tree limbs and shingles missing from some of the rooftops. A block before we turned into the street that circled around to the cul-de-sac we lived on we noticed some of the siding was ripped away from some of the houses and debris was covering the yards.

We turned on the circle that led to the court and the houses were in pretty bad shape. Windows were blown out and the houses had very little siding left on their exterior. Leo then started to turn on to the street where we lived. Across the road lay two large pillars head to head. The vehicle stopped and all of a sudden two of my neighbors both carrying shot guns came running around the bushes of home next to ours.

Rick was riding up front with Leo and they couldn't see Belinda and me sitting in the back of the van. They both started yelling "Stop! We're not going to let you through." I poked my head out from the back of the van and said what was going on. Fred the neighbor to the left of my house said its Mark let him through. Fred and Jim said they were afraid of looters and set the roadblock up in the front of the court. I told them thanks but please don't shoot anyone during the night.

There were only five houses that faced the cul-de-sac we lived on. There was no doubt that this was the hardest hit area in the addition. It looked like a war zone with timber, glass, shingles, and aluminum siding scattered all over the place. The house of the family who lived across from us had no roof and it was in my front yard. The upper roof of my tri-level was lying in the yard of the neighbor behind me. The three exterior walls of my two car attached garage were completely blown out and the roof had collapsed to the garage floor.

It was when I saw the condition of the house; my first thought of our dog Jessie began to surface. We kept her in the garage when we were gone, leaving the back door open to the fenced back yard. We all jumped out of the van and immediately started to kick around through the debris; there wasn't any sign of Jessie dead or alive. Jessie was extremely scared of storms and would be in my lap with the first loud clap of thunder.

We gave up our search for her and the house was definitely uninhabitable so we headed over to my sister's house. Jackie's house had only minimal damage with a few slates of siding and shingles missing. She invited all of us to camp out in her house that night, Belinda and I accepted, but Rick and Leo declined. Leo said he'd be back in the morning to help out.

The next morning Belinda, Jackie, her husband Tom, and I all got up at the crack of dawn. Jackie had made some coffee and poured them in to-go cups. We all then started to walk back over to the house.

We were just half way home and you could see our back yard, on the court behind the houses on the circle. All of a sudden darting over the broken down fences, Jessie came running at full speed. I've never seen her so excited to see me. To this day, I don't know how Jessie survived that storm.

I guess we were all fortunate the night of the storm. Usually it was our house that everyone gathered at instead of my brother's. In fact, in the whole addition there were only a few minor injuries due to the storm. There were probably more injuries in the aftermath, while people were trying to clean up and rebuild their homes.

Belinda and I went back to Jackie's house after we surveyed the house once more. I called our homeowner's insurance company and amazingly they sent someone out within the hour. The adjuster said it would be alright to remove the items left in the house.

We started making a lot of phone calls to see who could come over and help us salvage what was left of the personal items inside. I was quick in getting a rental truck and several of our friends and family volunteered space in their garages until we could rebuild.

We were extremely fortunate that our insurance company was a good one and didn't balk at paying off on the damage. We lost many items we were not inclined to repurchase. Rather we used that money to improve the house. We added a new front porch, a complete intercom and stereo system that ran throughout the house, and we added ceiling light fixtures to each of the rooms.

We took out a non-bearing wall to enlarge our family room and moved our washer and dryer hook ups to the basement level. We even had the foresight to transform the small bedroom into a nursery. We were able to do all this and still be the first ones on the court to be back in our home. Some of our neighbors took over eight months to rebuild while hassling with their insurance companies.

The day Belinda and I brought Todd home and to his new nursery was the best day of my life. I can't help but think of how good the Lord had been to me. While Belinda and I lost our home, we were given a better home. I was devastated when I was told I could never have a child of my own, but God's plan for me was to have Todd, and for that I am extremely grateful.

CHAPTER 4

When I awoke around six the following morning at the hospital, I was pretty sore and stiff. I think everything was starting to catch up with me. The shock and stress of Todd's condition and the lack of sleep was beginning to take its toll. Linda was nowhere in sight, but since she's always been an early riser; I figured she had gone somewhere to freshen up. Shortly thereafter she reappeared, having gone to call and check on her mother who suffers with numerous health issues. I walked down the hall to check on Todd. His cranial pressure reading had dropped to ten, making me feel confident that everything was going well.

Belinda decided to leave the hospital for a while to wrap up some details at the office and also to stop by her home to gather up some things to bring back to the hospital. I was surprised when she returned only two hours later. You see, one of the problems Belinda and I had while we were married was her dedication to her job. I wouldn't say it was the main reason for our break up, but it was definitely a contributing factor. It was my desire that Belinda be a stay-at-home mother --- something that was reinforced by the adoption agency. While Belinda did stay home with Todd for the first six months after his arrival, she decided she wanted to go back to work "part time." We fought about it for quite some time. In fact, I even offered to quit my job and stay home myself, but that didn't go over too well. I finally relented, and just as I figured, Belinda was back to work full time in a few months. It was also a frequent occurrence to have her tell me she was going into the office for a couple of hours on her day off only to have her spend the entire day and sometimes into the evening. So on this day I really expected her to be longer than just a couple of hours. I guess a lot had changed in the 17 years since our divorce.

Sitting in the waiting room I began to reflect back again; Todd was a very active baby and toddler. He didn't cry often and would generally sleep through the night. However, getting him to lie down and go to sleep was a different story.

One of us would place Todd in his crib around eight o'clock every evening. In the lower part of our tri-level home was the family room where we would we would turn on the intercom speaker and listen. All you could hear was a very happy baby having a good time in his crib. He'd laugh and talk gibberish for hours --- Belinda and I would just listen and laugh.

It didn't take long before Todd figured out ways he could climb out of his crib. At eight months he was pulling himself up on the sofa and standing. He was even taking a few steps, and when he finally got the hang of it, he really took off. He would endlessly run from one spot to another, laughing with every step.

As a toddler, Todd would get into everything. It wasn't uncommon to find him sitting in a kitchen cabinet, after strewing all the pots and pans on the floor. On one occasion I was caring for Todd in Belinda's absence. While watching a football game on television Todd was playing behind me with some of his toys. All of a sudden I heard the dogs barking in the back yard, by this time we had two dogs the second one named Frank, which was brought home by Belinda, but again it soon became my responsibility.

I got up from my lounge chair so I could check out the commotion outside and I noticed Todd was no longer playing behind me. Somehow Todd had crawled onto the sofa, pushed out the screen of a ground-level window and was playing in the back yard with our two dogs.

I thought the whole event was rather funny, but unfortunately Belinda didn't find it the least bit amusing. When I told her the story expecting a laugh, she in turn scolded me for not keeping a closer eye on Todd. I guess I will have to admit getting a little wrapped up in the ball game, but I still say I only turned my back for a minute and off he went.

Todd may have been a handful, but he's been the best thing that ever came into my life. I remembered how our friends and family would be amazed at Todd's hyperactivity. Belinda and I became so used to the way he ran around; we were almost oblivious to it. I can remember my brother Michael whose son Ryan was seven months older than Todd, commenting on Todd's behavior after watching him running from one end of the room to another. He asked, "Does he ever just sit down?"

I loved taking the day off and spending it with Todd. I would also volunteer to take care of Ryan on those days, so the two could play in the sandbox that I built in our back yard. It was so much fun watching them interact with each other. Ryan was kind of laid back and Todd just wanted to run and play. Ryan would build something out of blocks or sand and Todd would run by and destroy it.

You'd think I was living a very happy life --- I had a wife, a son, family, and good friends. I had a very nice home and a job I really enjoyed. Unfortunately, soon after Todd's arrival I lost my job and our marriage started to fall apart.

Belinda returned to the hospital around 10:00 AM that morning. Linda and I then decided we would go home and freshen up. We returned around 12:00 p.m. and as we were entering the hospital we ran into a couple of my friends leaving. They had just come from the fifth floor looking for me. Craig was a Lieutenant on the Indianapolis Police Department where I was currently employed as a civilian worker. Danny was the head of the department's credit union and a retired Deputy Chief.

I briefed Craig and Danny on Todd's condition, which hadn't changed since I talked to Craig on the phone yesterday. Craig was the only one in the department that I felt comfortable talking to, because he seemed to have a similar personality as mine. He knew I was hurting but knew I would want to keep my composure so he wouldn't press me for how I was feeling.

Another coworker had called earlier. My friend Bob had been diagnosed with muscular dystrophy at age eighteen and he was now forty-five. When I first met Bob eight years ago, he was able to take a few steps with a cane. Now he was completely dependent on his motorized cart to get around.

Bob and I had a unique friendship based on our love for our two sons. Todd was quite a bit older than Bob's son Robbie who lived in Dallas, Texas. To tell you the truth I don't remember if Todd and Robbie ever met. I can remember when I first met Bob. He had just recently been divorced and he took it pretty hard. He had a strong commitment to family as I did and couldn't understand why his wife wanted to be on her own. He, of course, blamed it on his handicap, but there was a lot more to it than that. Bob could be a handful even without his handicap; there are always two sides to the story when there is a divorce.

It was equally hard on Bob when his then ex-wife had to relocate to Dallas. I became Bob's shoulder during that time, for I understood his feelings of hopelessness more than any of his other friends. Since that time we would both discuss the joys and heartbreaks we had while raising our sons. I knew if I talked to Bob at this time I would break down in tears. This is something I didn't want to do in front of a waiting room full of people. Bob offered to come to the hospital, but I was glad that he understood why I rather he didn't.

When Craig and Danny left, Linda and I went back upstairs, and I checked on Todd. His cranial pressure was close to twenty. Due to the high reading I called in a member of the nursing staff informing her of my concern. She indicated it had been a while since his last dose of the medication. It was about two hours later, after administering yet another dosage, Todd's reading had again dropped back down to twelve.

It was Friday evening and the visitors' waiting room was packed. My sister and many of Belinda's relatives came by to visit and then left. Many family and friends of other patients remained way past the posted visiting hours. I remember wishing everyone would just leave so I could get some rest.

While waiting I sat next to Linda in silence. I thought back to the time when Todd was only a year old. It was about that time I was notified that my job was being eliminated due to the loss of government funding.

At that time, I was working for a company that distributed remedial reading and mathematical testing materials to most of the Indianapolis Public Schools. I would deliver the blank booklets, pick them up, grade the answers, and distribute token award gifts to the schools. It was the best and most rewarding job I had ever had. Previously, most of the work I had done was factory or assembly type.

The two ladies who ran the Parents in Touch program for this contracted company offered me the opportunity to retain my position by transferring me to Miami, Florida. However, because Belinda and I were still in the adoption process, we were unable to relocate. I guess I will have to admit that it was good that Belinda had returned to work. It helped get us through a couple of rough months while I drew unemployment and looked for another job.

I was out every day looking for employment when a neighbor and good friend told me to apply for a job with the City of Indianapolis. Fred has secured a job with the City's Administration division a couple of years ago and worked closely with that department's head. Fred had told me that he was always impressed with the way I worked hard around the house and saw that I often brought my work home with me. I applied for the job and with Fred's recommendation and strong influence I was able to secure a position with the City's Fleet Maintenance Division.

The job at the City's fleet was at first mainly clerical. My immediate supervisor liked me a lot, but the second in command of the division, seemed to have a problem with me. He was very gruff and though others in the department said he was like that with everyone, I felt he had it in for me.

It was a month after I started work at the fleet; Fred was able to give me some insight on the assistant administrator's problem. Supposedly he was campaigning for one of his friend's son to get the position I was hired to do and Fred's influence proved to be stronger than his.

Eventually, the assistant administrator acknowledged my work was good and lay off the bad attitude. Within six month's of working at the fleet my supervisor approached me with a supervisor position in the one of the fleet's part's room. It was a large increase in pay, but it took on a lot of responsibility. I didn't regret my decision to take the position, but I guess I started to complain about how hard the job was at home. Belinda one night at dinner made herself clear that she was tired of my complaining and didn't want to hear about my job anymore. I never brought up the subject again.

Though the job I had was pretty demanding I still enjoyed working with most of the people there. After a while I became familiar with my new position and was able to handle the pressure without bringing it home with me.

Coming home in the evening was still the highlight of my day. Since Belinda had gone back to work, I would pick Todd up from the babysitter's house and begin to make supper. That's right I would make the supper. Belinda would always work later than I would and to tell you the truth and I'm not bragging but was definitely a better cook. Sometimes making dinner and watching Todd could be quite challenging. When he wasn't trying to help, he was into something else that required my attention. Actually, I didn't mind a bit, Todd had a lot of energy and was a lot of fun to watch.

I really loved being a father --- Todd was such a blessing in every way. He was such a happy toddler and into everything. As a child growing up I lived close to a family with adopted children, and I remember wondering if their parents really loved them as much as my folks loved me. As Todd's father, I can certainly attest that no one could love a child more than I loved Todd. He was indeed my son.

Belinda and I began the process of adopting our second child within a few weeks after officially adopting Todd. Thus starting what we knew was going to be another two-year and a half-year process. While it would have appeared that all was well, the truth was things were not very pleasant at home or at work.

Saturday and Sunday at the hospital was an emotional roller coaster. Saturday morning we were informed they still hadn't been able to stabilize Todd's condition and they were going to place Todd into a drug induced coma.

Saturday night the catholic priest from Belinda's parish stopped by. Belinda filled him in on Todd's condition and asked if he should receive the last rites. Belinda felt it necessary and requested that the priest perform the sacrament. We all proceeded back to Todd's room and while the priest anointed Todd's forehead tears began to flow once again.

Between visitors on Sunday I had plenty of time to reflect back once again to the time when Belinda's and my marriage was on the rocks.

My job with the City of Indianapolis was not one I enjoyed and a couple of problems started up that brought back a lot of the pressure. Belinda and I had very little to say to each other and we were rapidly drifting apart. I knew for quite some time that Belinda was not happy in our relationship but decided to avoid confrontation. I was so afraid of losing all that I had --- my family, friends (most of which were Belinda's family), the house. Additionally, I was raised to believe that divorce was not acceptable, except in extreme cases.

Belinda kept distancing herself from me and I frequently asked her if we had a problem. She would always hesitate and then reply no. Although I accepted her answer, I knew she wasn't being honest with me. I, of course, didn't really want to know the truth, which meant I wasn't being honest with myself either.

Todd was only three and a half years old when I could no longer stand the silence and Belinda's coldness towards me. I had noticed for a number of months that Belinda would place her wedding rings on the sink when doing dishes and fail to put them back on when the dishes were done. I would pick them up and hand them to her and she would fiddle with them and finally place them back on her finger. It was after one of those times that she was extremely reluctant to put the rings on, that I forced the issue. I told her I'd had enough and that we needed to settle this once and for all. After waiting for what seemed to be an eternity for an answer, I finally asked if she wanted a divorce. Still she gave no answer, but in her silence I knew that Belinda indeed, wanted a divorce.

CHAPTER 5

I'm having trouble keeping track of the days. I believe four days have passed and it is now day five and the start of new week. I didn't realize this was Labor Day, until I called Craig at work. Many officers had to work on the holidays though Craig usually wasn't one of them. The lieutenant had an administrative job and headed up the Planning and Research area of the department.

Craig told me he had a lot of work to catch up on and the best time to do it was while most of police headquarters was empty. I updated him on Todd's condition and what had transpired over the weekend. I asked him to fill in Bob, and everyone else who might be concerned.

After talking to Craig, I turned to Linda and told her I was going for a walk. Walking is something I did when I needed to calm my anxieties. Linda asked if she should come along and I said no. I wanted to be by myself for a few minutes. She asked, if it would be okay for her to run over to her office for awhile to check up on few things. I told her to go ahead and that I would be all right.

I walked out the front door of the hospital and for the first time I busted into tears. I had completely lost track of time and Craig had reminded me of what day it was. Yesterday was the day Todd and I were supposed to have made our annual trek to Enochsburgh with the rest of my immediate family.

Labor Day weekend was something we all looked forward to, especially my father. Enochsburg is a small town sixty miles southeast of Indianapolis. The town consisted of a church, school, a small restaurant, which is only open on Wednesdays, Fridays, and Saturdays, and a few houses.

This small community located in southeast Indiana is part of a large German settlement, including such towns as Batesville, Oldenburgh, and Hamburg. My father's side of the family all originated from that area and his father was only twelve years old when his mother moved to Indianapolis. In the cemetery across the street from the old limestone church is the grave of my great grandfather George, a German stonemason who had settled in this small community.

St. John's church would have a picnic every Labor Day and the fried chicken dinner was the big draw. I can remember when my brother, sisters, and I were kids we couldn't wait for dad and mom to get up from dinner and let us go to the fish pond booth. Grandma and Grandpa would ride down with us and Grandma would give us each a dollar to spend. The fishpond consisted made up of a wash tub filled with water and floating plastic fish. You donated a dime and the attendant would hand you a small net. You would then lift a fish out of the water and the attendant would check the number written on its bottom. You then won the corresponding prize.

That tradition went on to the next generation with Todd, and his cousins Ryan and Jon, being the anxious kids. The gifts were only small plastic whistles or animal figures, but once in awhile you would pick out a grand prize of a yo-yo, paddleball, or small airplane kit made of balsa wood.

When the boys got older it was the chicken dinner that became the draw. They would fix mashed potatoes, corn, green beans, dressing, and some of the best fried chicken I've ever had. The Indiana home grown tomatoes were also to die for.

Todd and I would always look forward to that day and we had just discussed it the day of the accident. I had called him to let him know what time I was going to pick him up from his mother's. He let me know he would drive over to my house and we could leave from there. He also said he would call me tomorrow after work, because he wanted to come over and work on his car stereo.

I can't remember when I last missed the picnic and it was only the second time that Todd had missed it in his life. The first time being just last year for reasons I'll get into later.

I walked around the hospital, which is one of, if not the biggest hospital in the city. I always favored St. Francis Hospital in Beech Grove, not only because it was closer to home, but because I worked there as a dishwasher during my junior and senior years of high school. I will admit though I was very impressed with the dedication of the nursing and other staff members at Methodist. I felt very encouraged by their diligence and professionalism.

As I walked I tried not to make eye contact with the cars passing by on the busy streets surrounding the hospital. The burst of tears I shed earlier did help relieve some of my anxiety, but occasionally a tear would roll down my cheek. I kept picturing Todd lying up there with all of the tubes and wires hanging around him.

Returning to the hospital, I didn't go back up to the room right away. I went to the cafeteria and got something to drink. I exited through a door that led outside into a courtyard area completely surrounded by the hospital. I just didn't want to go back to that fifth floor waiting room for awhile, it was really starting to close in on me.

I can't tell you how long I was sitting there when a couple of friends from my past sat down beside me. Mike and Jane Simms had a dual connection to me. Mike was Leo's older brother, the friend who introduced me to Belinda. Jane his wife was the sister of a high school classmate. Mike too, of course, was Belinda's first cousin.

They were there visiting one of Jane's sisters-in-law who had an ongoing health problem. I believe it was a respiratory problem but I can't be sure. They had heard of Todd's accident and had already stopped by the waiting room on Saturday to check on Belinda. Today they saw me through one of the hospital's glass doors and came over to check on me.

Jane had asked me how I was holding up. I told her I was fine and just had to get away for a moment. Mike asked, "Aren't you cold sitting here?" Until Mike asked I hadn't noticed that it was a bit chilly out here. The wind was blowing, the clouds were thick, and there was a slight drizzle of rain starting to fall. I looked around and realized there wasn't anyone but us sitting in the courtyard.

Of all of Belinda's relatives, I probably saw Mike and Jane the most since our divorce. Their son was Todd's age and they both attended Roncalli High School together. Todd and Mike Jr. both played several sports and would often compete against each other while attending separate grade schools. There would also be several times where Mike's and Todd's schools would compete before or after Todd's team and I would spend some time talking to Mike and Jane.

I could tell that I must have looked pretty pathetic worried over Todd's condition. Mike and Jane were both very concerned about my sitting out there all by myself. We chatted a little and Jane thought it was time to go back inside to warm up. I walked with them to the hospital parking garage where they departed to go home. I went back into the hospital lobby area and sat down leaning my head back on the chair. I still wasn't ready to go back to that depressing and cramped waiting room.

The lobby's lounge area had some very nice comfortable chairs. I knew Linda wouldn't' be back for at least a couple of hours so I remained there deep in thought and prayer.

I can always remember setting some time aside for prayer every day of my life. It was usually in the evening just prior to falling asleep. In the past few years I've been praying a little more often. I wish I had done more of it during the time I was going through the divorce with Todd's mother. I thought I knew everything and could deal with anything. I was sadly mistaken. When Belinda first told me she wanted a divorce, I broke down and cried like a baby. I just felt I had lost everything, my son, my home, and most of my friends that were Belinda's relatives.

My parents had been married over thirty-five years. My older sister and her husband for twelve, my brother nine, and Belinda and I would have been married for ten years in just a couple of months. All of my Christian background and training taught me that divorce wasn't an option. I always believed that there were only two acceptable reasons for a divorce. No one should have to be involved with an abusive spouse, and I know I wouldn't be able to stay with an unfaithful wife. I look back now and see how idealistic I must have been.

I left the house and stayed at Mom and Dad's while Belinda and Todd stayed at the house. Belinda said, "She'd find a place real soon and move out." It only took her a month to find an apartment, and I moved back into the house. I still remember walking back into the mostly empty house and breaking down into uncontrollable tears. I had told Belinda to take what ever she needed and she certainly did.

I walked through the mostly empty house and couldn't believe this was happening. When the 1978 tornado hit it was quite a shock, but it held no comparison. The worst part was sitting in my lounge chair thinking that Todd was no longer in the house. All I could think about is how he would sit in my lap and I would read him a story. Our favorite was The *Cat and the Hat*, by Dr. Seuss. I read him that book so often that I almost had it memorized.

Todd and I would play with his little toy Hot Wheels and have a blast crashing them together from a few feet apart. He was such a loving child and just laughed all the time. I couldn't help but feel that I would never be able to share those times again.

I wish I had known then what I know now and been a stronger individual back then. I must have thought by giving Belinda everything she would think I was a great guy and come running back to me. I was wrong and I should have just let her go and demanded that Todd remain with me.

It didn't take long for the news to leak out that Belinda and I were having marital problems. I think our family and friends were just as shocked as I was. At least I had indications that there was something very wrong. Even before I had moved back to the house several people had called to find out what was wrong and asked what they could do. Several of them suggested we seek counseling and I, of course, I was all for it.

I approached Belinda on the subject and at first she didn't want any part of it. After a while she relented under the pressure from both of our families and mutual friends. By the time we finally went to the counselor's office I was a wreck, for I was definitely having a nervous breakdown.

I met Belinda outside the office and she acted as cold as ice. We went inside and sat on opposite sides of the waiting room. I was pretty excited about meeting with the counselor for I had worked out what I was going to say to him over and over again in my mind. I was going to tell him about what I thought were all our problems and then tell him I was willing to work hard to put our marriage back together. I just knew the marriage counselor was going to fix everything and I was going to be happy again.

We waited quite some time until a young man came out and escorted us back to his office. His first question was, "what could he do for us." I don't remember what I said, but I'm sure it was quite incoherent, since my mind was in a constant state of confusion.

He listened graciously and turned to Belinda and asked what she expected from us seeing him. She told him flat out, "Nothing: I don't even want to be here." The counselor stood up and said, "Well that's it then: if you don't want to be here then there is nothing I can do."

That was the end of the meeting and Belinda got up and left and I just sat there with a shocked look on my face. The counselor tried to explain to me what just happened, but I was totally out of it. I believe that was the first time I really got mad since our split. Before that moment, I was too busy feeling sorry for myself and blaming myself for everything. Here I was willing to do whatever was necessary to save our marriage, but she wasn't even willing to try.

I believe it was at that point I realized that my marriage was over. I almost felt relieved, and as time wore on I was very glad that Belinda had stuck to her guns. It was terrible living in a loveless marriage. Towards the end Belinda made it clear that I was nothing to her and she treated me that way. We were totally different people with different ideals.

I think it's important to understand that this is my version of the events that led to our divorce. Like I said earlier, there are always two sides to a divorce and I'm sure Belinda could spin a completely different version. In a way, it later became the best thing that could have happen to me. After several years of ups and downs I finally met Linda, which has been a true blessing in my life. Yet I still wonder what emotional effect our divorce had on Todd?

I would like to say that my bout with depression and anxiety was over when I realized my marriage was over, unfortunately that was not the case. I had given up on trying to restore the marriage, but I wasn't willing to give up my son. Belinda and I both fought for full custody and it seemed she won every battle. After several months of lawyers, counselors and court sessions I finally relented to have joint legal custody. I had made one big mistake and that was to allow Belinda to take Todd with her when we initially spilt. Fathers weren't given custody of children back then as often as mother's unless they were proven unfit plus the fact that she already had physical custody of Todd, my battle was futile.

I was pretty bad off during the whole proceedings. By the time we had our final court date, I had pretty much resigned myself to be a part time father. A court ordered counselor had recommended Belinda and I work on a joint legal custody agreement. Belinda and I met one afternoon and discussed what each other's role would be.

She agreed to allow me joint legal custody, which meant that Todd would live with her, but I would have an equal voice in his upbringing.

I told her since my health insurance benefits were better than hers; I would continue to carry the family plan. This was a decision that I later regretted. First of all Belinda interpreted that to mean I'd pay for all of Todd's medical expenses, which I later informed her that wasn't going to be the case. The insurance agreement also became a problem when the family coverage became a whole lot more expensive than the single coverage, but I was committed to our agreement.

When we discussed these items regarding our roles on raising Todd neither of us took notes. I had brought a list of things I wanted to address and we covered his schooling and agreed to send him through the parochial school system each paying half his tuition. I told Belinda she could choose a school near to her new residence.

Trying to decide how much time Todd would be spending at each other's homes brought on the greatest debate. We finally decided on every other weekend he would spend at my house, but it would be a three-day weekend starting on Friday evening and returning on Monday.

Later I felt that wasn't quite fair and I requested an additional day, which Belinda at first wouldn't concede. I think someone beside myself, must have convinced her to allow me the extra day. She came over one night to pick up Todd from my house and said she'd let me have the extra time if she could have the stereo. I said, "Take it."

I knew that Belinda's intention was to let me have Todd that extra day, but she figured she might as well profit from it too. What was nice about that little dispute was the stereo system broke a week after she got it.

By the time the final court date was set Belinda and I had agreed verbally on everything. When I arrived at court that day, my anxiety was as high as ever. I couldn't wait for the divorce settlement hearing to be over.

I sat with my attorney and the judge entered the courtroom. When the judge asked if there was anything any one wanted to say, I got the shock of my life. At her attorney's urging Belinda stood up in courtroom and demanded full custody and a better financial settlement. Everything we had verbally agreed on was now null and void.

CHAPTER 6

Linda arrived back from the office while I was still sitting in the lobby. She asked if I was all right and I just nodded in the affirmative. Together we went back upstairs to the waiting room and continued our vigil. I waited till the regular visiting hours and walked back through the corridors to see Todd. I'd never lingered long; I just couldn't stand watching his chest rising up and down as the machine pumped air into his lungs. I'd touch his hand or arm and they would feel warm, but also felt hard and leathery. I'd say a little prayer and asked the Lord to be with him.

It being a holiday my sister Clare and more of Belinda's family came to visit. Belinda's brother Tim and his wife Debbie spent a good portion of the day there. Tim talked to me for quite some time. We were discussing some brake problems he was having. I think it's been four days now "camping out" in a hospital that all the conversation seemed to revolve around Todd's condition or someone else's ailment. I appreciated the diversion talking about Tim's brake job, which briefly reminded me there was another world going on outside this waiting room.

All weekend long family and friends of other critical care unit patients had streamed in and out of the visiting room. The family of the young teens injured by their all-terrain vehicles that had flipped and rolled had at least some good news: one of the boy's injuries improved over night and was moved to a regular room in a different part of the hospital. The other one's condition had stabilized but hadn't improved enough to be moved.

It's so strange to be placed in this type of environment. I've been very fortunate until now that I hadn't had very much experience in this type of situation. When Todd was around twelve or so, he came crawling out of his bedroom in terrible pain. He doubled over and said his side was killing him. I didn't panic, because Todd was famous for his over dramatization of pain. Whenever he got hit with a ball or sprained an ankle he wouldn't cry, but would roll around holding the injured limb. It was his way of saying, "Look at me; I'm hurt."

This time though, he seemed even more dramatic than ever so I decided to take him to the emergency room. I called his mother and sat with him waiting for his mother to arrive. All the time he was wrenching in pain and yelling how much it hurt. The doctor diagnosed an appendicitis and said they needed to operate right away.

A nurse gave him some morphine to ease his pain while they made preparations to operate. The morphine had just kicked in when his mother arrived. It was almost comical to see the difference the morphine made. For over an hour Todd had been screaming about the pain and he couldn't stand it. Once the morphine took effect Todd's agonizing pain had turned him into a smiling "Hi mom, what's happening," kind of guy.

It wasn't but a few minutes after his mother arrived that they took Todd into surgery. The operation went without a hitch and he would soon be back to his old self. Todd asked if he would get to eat a lot of ice cream and I told him that was for tonsillitis not appendicitis.

The circumstances in this situation of Todd being in critical condition were quite different than the appendicitis episode. Belinda and I were concerned about Todd being operated on, but we knew that the appendectomy was common place and the doctor's assured us that there shouldn't be any problem. We didn't have that kind of assurance this time; in fact, I don't believe the doctor or staff ever gave us a positive report.

The day wore on at the hospital and evening once again came to pass. Todd's condition was just about the same; I had mistakenly assumed maybe his injury had stabilized. Belinda and I discussed that one of us might consider going home to get some rest. We knew that one of us should stay just in case there was a problem during the night. Belinda wasn't willing to leave so Linda and I went home. Not before I made Belinda promise to call me if anything went wrong during the night.

That evening I lay down in my bed for the first time in five nights. I looked at Todd's picture on the dresser of my room and again my mind reverted back to a much happier time.

The court saw through Belinda's attorney's ploy and granted me joint legal custody. I lost out on some of the financial settlement, but at that point I was tired and wanted to start rebuilding my life. I'm not holding a grudge against Todd's mother that is all water under the bridge now. I'm sure Belinda could add some equal criticism about me. We had our battles over the years, but I would guess they were fewer than most divorced couples trying to raise children.

I only remember these things because the divorce was a very traumatic experience for me. I grew a lot during that time and decided to make some changes in my life. The main thing was I wasn't going to worry about things as much or try to control every aspect of my life.

Even before the divorce was over, I decided to keep the house we were living in. I borrowed some money and paid Belinda her half of the home's equity. Todd had his old room when he came for visits. The visitation settlement was just as Belinda and I had agreed on earlier. Once every two weeks starting on Friday I would pick Todd up and I would return him to the baby sitter's, his mom's, or school on the following Tuesday morning.

Fortunately that wasn't the full extent of my time with Todd though. Belinda was at first reluctant to call me to baby sit Todd, instead she would call one of her sister's, when she had other things to do. I figured Belinda thought I would use her absence against her in the future. I let her know that wasn't the case and she then started to call me quite often to come pick up Todd.

I also attended every one of Todd's school functions and sporting events. I attended his weekly gymnastic and dance classes when he was very young and in which he struggled. Yet we encouraged him as much as possible. As he got older I coached him in Little League starting in the peewees all the way up through the majors. When Todd reached the Pony League the coaching staff was already established so I decided to become just a spectator.

I had made up my mind that I was going to be an active father in my son's life. I may not have been with him every day, but I would make best of the time we had together.

I will admit one thing though, that first year was tough. I no longer wanted anything to do with Belinda. The hurt ran deep, not with her divorcing me, it was because of her betrayal. I felt I didn't deserve the treatment I got in the courtroom. Belinda justified it by saying she was just looking out for "number one.' This was a very popular saying back then especially with the "me generation."

I still remember that first year after the separation; tears would well up in my eyes each time I would drop Todd off at the baby sitter. It was also very hard coming home to that empty house each night on those days. I'd make his bed and pick up a few errant toys. I'd sit in my easy chair and pick up a book half heartily flipping through the pages.

It took some time for me to adjust to my new circumstance and I can't tell you exactly when I did. I believe it was towards the end of the divorce proceedings that I was such a basket case I went to the emergency ward of St. Francis hospital and tried to get them to admit me.

I told them I just needed some rest; I didn't want to fight anymore. You see the divorce wasn't the only thing I was battling at the time. As a supervisor at the City's Fleet and in charge of the vehicle parts room I was in the middle of a criminal investigation. Two of the men working for me were stealing the place blind and reselling auto parts on the streets. There was a grand jury investigation and though it was quite informal, it nearly drove me over the edge. I'm sure the investigators thought I was a nut case, and I was, because I think I answered every question with I don't know or I'm not sure. I think I was the most scared during the time when one of the thieves tried to say I told them to falsify some records. This of course indicated I had something to do with the thefts. I believe this allegation shocked me back to reality where I could prove my innocence. My biggest mistake was being gullible and believing the two men. They stole the auto parts and when caught, they lied and tried to pass the blame on to someone else. I learned a great deal about trust during that time.

When I went to the hospital for help, the doctors at the emergency room tried to convince me that staying at the hospital wasn't the answer. It didn't matter how much they protested, I wasn't going anywhere until I was better. Finally one of the nurses asked me if I had any children and the question struck me like a brick had just hit me between the eyes. I remembered that this was Friday and I was to pick up Todd from the babysitter that afternoon. I sat up on the gurney I was lying on and said "I have to go get my son. "

The emergency room staff was concerned and asked if I was alright. To tell you the truth I really didn't know; I just knew I had to go get Todd. My responsibility as a father took precedent over my problems and I had a new priority. I suddenly realized there wasn't going to be a quick fix to my problems and I knew I had to continue on. I think, it was during that time I gave up depending on my own resources and started to turn the bigger problems I faced over to the Lord.

I can look back now and see how Todd had been an important part of my healing. If it hadn't been for my responsibility to him and the strength of the Lord, I don't know if I could have walked out of that emergency room. I learned a lot during that time. One thing was I couldn't control everything in my life. Secondly, it was important to take one day at a time. When I was at my worst, all I could see was the worst in everything. I can only advise people who have had to go through that type of agony to hang in there. If you do I can guarantee you there will be better days ahead.

It turned out that the divorce was one of the best things that ever happened to me. It made me grow up and face reality. I can remember Leo, as a friend, saying to me, "I was too idealistic." He was right. It's not a perfect world and we have to learn to adjust. Everyone is not going to agree with you on everything and you're not going to make everyone believe the same way you do. I'm not saying you shouldn't fight for what you believe in, but you should also recognize your limitations.

I mentioned earlier there were some happy times and that was the time I spent with Todd. We always had a blast playing football downstairs in the family room. I would push all the furniture to one side and he'd line up at one end of the long room. I would be at the other end of the room and the couch was behind me. I'd throw him the ball and he'd come running. I'd tackle him a couple of times and then would let him get around me on third down. When he'd get close to the couch Todd would do a flying leap into the end zone. We'd both laugh and start again this time he would kick the Nerf football off to me. I'd always be on my knees and he'd jump on me for the tackle.

I will never understand the mentality of a divorced parent who deserts their children. When I became a non-custodial parent I decided I was going to insert myself in every way possible into Todd's life. I also wanted to support Todd financially too; that is something Bob, my handicap friend, and I would always agree on. Here was Bob, a man who had muscular dystrophy so severe he could have been on disability a long time ago. Yet, he wouldn't hear of it, he wanted to be able to give as much as he could to help raise his son. I don't believe a lot of absent parents realize how rewarding it is to remain a part of your child's life.

I know Bob would never turn his back on his son, but if he did I'm sure he would have quit working five years ago. I can remember Bob calling me one night saying the doctors told him he had two years to live. Bob was crying, but he wasn't concerned for his own well being, but for Robbie. He didn't want his son growing up not having a father. He also wanted to see Robbie grow up. I sincerely believe that Bob would have met the doctor's morbid prediction if it weren't for his love for his son. Bob's health has declined over the years, but he's still working and is still very much enjoying his time with his son. It's been six years since the doctor predicted his two-year fate.

I, too, enjoyed my time with Todd. When Todd started to take gymnastics / dance lessons I would always attend even when it wasn't on my scheduled days. I don't think Todd really enjoyed the class but went just to please his mother and I. He'd try real hard, but just lacked the talent and coordination.

There was one boy in the class that was really good and could do back flips, hand stands, and mid air somersaults. Todd really got frustrated when he couldn't perform as well. I believed he felt it was his fault he couldn't do some of the stunts and not his lack of God given talent that the other boy possessed.

Hot wheels and G. I. Joe's had been Todd's favorite toys. He had both the Hot Wheel's service station and racetrack. Todd and I would take turns picking out our favorite cars and then we'd have them flying everywhere. Later I bought him one of the glow in the dark electric tracks that climbed the wall. We would race the cars together and he'd win almost every time despite my best efforts.

Todd's G. I. Joe collection was by far his favorite plaything. He'd spend hours setting up tanks, jeeps, guns, and men on both sides of the room. Sometimes he'd let me take command of one side and he'd take the other. What took hours for him to set up took just a couple of minutes for us to destroy. We'd start out real slow, maybe hitting one tank with a "bomb," and then it would escalate to a brawl. Men and vehicles would fly everywhere. When we were finished "blowing up" the world, he would stand up and yell, "Here I come." He would then leap on me and we'd wrestle around on the floor.

Those memories of Todd's toddler years will always be precious to me. I've kept all of his G. I. Joe's and Hot Wheels safely tucked away in the attic. I've been saving them for when he gets a family of his own. I figure when Todd finally settles down and begins to have kids of his own he'll appreciate having his old toys.

One of the things I missed from Todd's toddler years was him sitting on my lap while we watched television or when I read him a story. He learned the "ins and outs" of football at an early age and would enjoy watching the Chicago Bears with me. Walter Payton would get the ball and Todd would just be amazed by his performance.

CHAPTER 7

It is now day six, Linda and I arrived back at the hospital around 6:00 am. I must have been exhausted, because I slept really well that night. I woke up refreshed and ready to spend another grueling day in the waiting room. Todd's mother was already awake when we arrived. She said, "Todd had a problem a couple of hours earlier, but she didn't know the details. Supposedly, the nurses said they were trying to control the problem by adjusting his medicine. I asked her why she didn't call me and she said she would have if things would have worsened.

I went back immediately to see him and I was pleasantly surprised to see the brain pressure monitor registering around eight or nine. This was very encouraging to me and I felt he was starting to recover. Belinda's brother Tim and his wife Debbie came again to visit early this morning. Debbie was a registered nurse and at one time had been assigned to a critical care unit similar to this one.

Debbie went back to Todd's room and was able to take a look at his charts. She came back and was discouraged by what she read. Debbie said she has seen this before and told us not to get our hopes up. She then went down the hall to talk with some of the hospital's nursing staff and returned a little more optimistic.

According to Todd's attending staff there had been vast improvements in technology over the years since Debbie was in this type of unit. His chances of recovery may not be as bad as she had first indicated. Tim and Debbie were both nice people and I always thought highly of them. I also respected and appreciated Debbie's input.

My second visit of the day to Todd's room was less encouraging. In fact, my hopes were again dashed when the digits on his monitor read eighteen. Once again I voiced my concerns to the nurses. They told me they had just administered another dose of his medicine and the readings should improve soon. This time I didn't take comfort from what the nurse said. I started to wonder why the brain pressure was still fluctuating and why they couldn't get it under control by now. I felt as if I was on a roller coaster of emotions the last few days and this was another major down time.

Linda had gone into work that morning and had dropped me off at the hospital. She had not planned to stay long, but she wanted to get a few things caught up at the office. It was about eleven and Linda hadn't come back yet, so I took another one of my now regular walks around the hospital. All I could think about was Todd and how much fun we had especially back at the old house.

Even when Todd wasn't staying at my house I remember how he used to call and tell me all the things he had done that day. He would be so excited when he accomplished something and couldn't wait to talk to me. I would receive the calls with mixed emotions. It was nice knowing he wanted to share those events with me, but I was sad not to have been part of the moment.

Fortunately, I did have a few of those moments at my house too. One of my favorite times was when he first learned how to ride his bike without his training wheels.

Our house was located on a cul-de-sac with ample room to practice without any traffic. I had taken the training wheels off his bike at his request, since according to him he was a big boy now. I took him out on the court and held on to the back of the seat to steady him as he peddled. As soon as I let go of the seat, Todd wouldn't get far and would land hard on the concrete.

I was very proud of the way; he never cried or gave up. He scraped his knees several times and unlike his dramatic nature towards injuries he'd get back up and jump right back on the bike.

We tried this method of holding on to his seat for about fifteen minutes and Todd decided he wanted to try doing it on his own. So I sat on the front porch and became an observer shouting words of encouragement.

He tried and tried for about an hour, always falling after a few feet then jumping back up and trying again. Finally after countless tries, he just took off and after that there was no stopping him. He was smiling from ear to ear, yelling "look dad I'm riding it." I had never been as proud of him as I was then. He worked very hard and was determined to ride that bike and darn if he didn't do it on his own. I will always cherish that moment and several others that came along as Todd grew up.

Todd was extremely quick witted too and very funny at times. Todd was only five or six years old when he started Peewee Little League. At the beginning of every game they would play the National Anthem and when it was over the announcer would bellow over the loud speaker PLAAAY BAAALL.

My brother Michael and I and the boys were visiting at mom and dad's house on July 3rd after Todd's first season of Little League. Beech Grove was having their Fourth of July fireworks display at the city park that evening so Michael decided to take Todd,

Ryan, and Jon down to the park to watch. I stayed at the house with mom and dad where we could see some of the fireworks from across the street.

Michael brought the boys back after the show around an hour later. He looked at me and said I was about to kill your boy down there. I asked why, what did he do now? He said nothing really, but after they played the National Anthem down at the park, Todd yelled out at the top of his lungs PLAAY BAAALL.

Todd was very good at imitating people also. He could do Howard Cossell really well and he would also do a great Dick Vitale "BOOM BABY" when he watched a Pacer basketball game.

I can honestly say that some of the best times Todd and I had we're spent traveling on vacations.

The time we went to California on a three-week road trip was probably the happiest time of our lives. I had packed our bags into the new 1991 Escort the night before we left. It was the first of June and Todd had just yesterday attended his last day of school for the summer break. I always like to start early in the morning when leaving on a trip and it was only five o'clock when we hit the road. I had to pretty much drag Todd out to the car with his pillow and he slept soundly in the back seat for at least a couple of hours.

I had taken a trip out West once before with Todd's mother before he was born. We had gone the direct route taking I70 to St. Louis, I 44 to Oklahoma City, and I40 all the way to Bakersfield California which was close to our destination of Lancaster where my aunt and uncle and my cousins lived nearby.

This time I decided to take a different route, because I'm always looking to see something new on every trip. We still took I70 to St. Louis but instead of going south on I44 we kept on I70 headed due west. I believe it was the most educational trip that Todd and I had ever been on. I can still picture the rolling hills and grasslands of Kansas, and the majestic snowcaps of the Rocky Mountains in Colorado.

Just inside the Utah border we headed South on Highway 191 to Arches National Park. Todd and I had a ball hiking up to the base of several of the parks beautiful natural stone arches. We traveled still further south on 191 through Monument Valley where several western movies and endless commercials were filmed. The rock formations were just unreal, but nothing compared to our next stop the north rim of the Grand Canyon.

We spent the night at one of the cabins in the park so we took advantage of seeing both the sunset and sunrise over the canyon. I've never seen a more magnificent sight in my life. I still remember Todd's reaction when we hiked to the canyon edge and he was able to see its vastness for the first time. His eyes got real big and said, "Whoa! This is unreal."

I can remember watching storm clouds miles away approaching us from the west. The dark clouds rolled quickly through the canyon and Todd and I rushed to our cabin. There wasn't a television or radio in sight, so we turned on the lights and Todd and I played a game of cards. The storm passed quickly so Todd and I headed back to the rim. Within a few minutes a tour guide came by with five or six people and asked if we wanted to join them. We took up the offer and Todd and I got a great education. You can see something like the Grand Canyon on television, but you haven't really seen it until you visit it in person.

Early the next morning after we watched the sunrise, Todd and I left the north rim and decided to check out the more popular and touristy south rim of the Canyon. It took several hours to drive back east to the Glen Canyon Dam and then west to the south rim, but it was worth the trip.

We stayed in the small town of Williams, Arizona on I-40 then headed west to Las Vegas, Nevada where we spent three nights and two days. I think it was Todd's favorite part of the trip. We stayed at the Excalibur Hotel where we attended the show, Knights of the Round Table. Later that night we would walk up and down the strip and both Todd and I were impressed with the volcano fountain in front of the Mirage Hotel. During the day we played miniature golf and went to the Circus Circus Hotel to eat lunch at the buffet and briefly watched the animals and trapeze act. I can remember walking out of the Circus Circus to the parking garage in search of our car. We went to third floor of the garage where I knew I had parked the car and started to panic when we discovered it wasn't where I thought it was. Most of our belongings were still in the trunk of the car and some of my money for the trip. Todd and I started to walk up and down the garage's ramp system to every floor hoping I'd mistaken where I parked it.

I finally gave up and decided it was time to call the police. We walked out the front of the garage and headed back to the hotel when Todd shouted out, "Look."

Right next door there was another garage that looked exactly like the one we just left. We ran over to it and ran up three flights of stairs and low and behold there was our car. I don't think I'd ever felt more relieved in my life as I felt at that moment.

From Vegas we traveled through the desert and on to Lancaster, California where my Aunt and Uncle still lived. We stayed only one night there and traveled down to Van Nuys, a small suburb in the San Fernando Valley near Los Angeles.

My Aunt Jenny and her daughter Pam lived there and we stayed a couple of nights with them. Pam took us on a tour of the area, which included Beverly Hills and Hollywood. She offered to take us to Disneyland, but Todd and I had visited Disney World the previous summer. She then decided to take us to Universal Studios and it turned out to be one of the highlights of the trip.

Todd and I left extremely early the next day, because my cousin Pam had scared me to death on the California Freeways the day before. I was amazed at the way she would dart in and out of lanes, but no more than how other California drivers were doing the same thing. I decided to get out of the area as fast I could, before this hick from Indiana met the L.A. rush hour.

Our next stop was to visit my two cousins who had moved from the Lancaster area to San Diego and Escondido. While in that area we went to the beach, but we were warned not to go swimming, because of polluted waters. Not that it mattered much, since it was a lot colder in San Diego than at home in Indiana. In fact, with the exception of Las Vegas, the whole trip was very cold and I told Todd that all we needed to pack was shorts. It was the first week of June and it was only fifty degrees.

My two cousins showed us all the sites. We checked out Sea World but didn't stay long. It wasn't just cold but it was also raining that day. The day we went to the San Diego Zoo and wild life preserve it was still cool but the sun was shining. Watching the animals in the preserve was something Todd and I enjoyed immensely.

The day we were planning to leave early my cousins decided we needed to stay a little longer and scheduled a Padres game in the early afternoon. I decided to accept the offer and marked off one of our planned stops on the way home, the old federal prison in Yuma, Arizona.

We only made one stop on our trip back home, the Carlsbad Caverns in New Mexico. Todd was impressed, but like me, was anxious to get home. Originally we planned to spend the night in the area to watch the bat flight that night but since we had several hours before evening we decided to push on.

We traveled on Interstate10 to El Paso where I pointed out to Todd the shanties on the Mexican side of the Rio Grande. It gave me the opportunity to point out to Todd how nice we had it and how we shouldn't complain about the little things.

When we were just outside of St. Louis I guess I wasn't paying attention to my speed as I was coming down a hill. A sheriff's car was sitting around a bend and they clocked me going twelve miles over the speed limit.

I pulled over and one of the deputies gruffly asked me to get out of the car and walk back to the officer that was standing in front of the patrol car. The deputy followed me back there and asked what the boy in the passenger side of the car hid under his seat as we pulled over. I told him I didn't know what he was talking about since I didn't notice him putting anything under there. The deputy then requested that I let them search my car. I didn't have anything to hide so I told him to go ahead.

I stood back with the other officer who was extremely friendly compared to his counterpart who began searching the car. He asked Todd several questions about where we've been and what he hid under his seat. Todd told him it was just one of his toys. The officer told Todd to get out the car while he looked under the seat. The deputy didn't find anything incriminating there and proceeded to search the trunk of the car. He actually pulled out every suitcase and bag out of the trunk, which was quite full of souvenirs by that point and searched each one thoroughly. In the meantime I was carrying on a conversation with the other deputy and he informed me that this highway was main artery for drug trafficking. He then gave me a couple of St. Louis baseball cards to give to Todd and politely gave me a ticket for speeding.

I can't complain, because they were just doing their job and they did it right. I was speeding and I gave them permission to search my car.

That was a great vacation, and I must say that was a year that Todd would never forget. He had already traveled to Florida with his mom in February and later in the summer his Boy Scout troop took a week and traveled to Niagara Falls and through parts of Canada.

Todd and I took our last trip together when he was fifteen years old. We went to the Six Flags Amusement Park just outside of St. Louis and then on to Branson, Missouri. Branson is an entertainment town with shows and amusement parks. Some believe it's all geared towards country music, but that is far from the truth.

Yes, there is a great representation of country artists there, but there are also magic acts, comedians, and other popular musicians there too. I'm not a country music fan myself and I knew Todd wasn't, but we had a blast playing miniature golf and catching some of the shows. We did decide to see one country group that was playing there the Oakridge Boys. I thought Todd would like it since he loved the Elvira song when he was little. When I told him I had tickets to the show he about threw a fit. I'm not going to see someone singing country music; I'll just wait for you back at the hotel. Of course I drug him to it and I can still remember him laughing like crazy at the jokes the Oakridge boys told during the show. I even think I saw Todd smiling listening to the music especially when they played Elvira.

All of the vacations were fantastic with the exception of one, which I won't go into right now. I just want to reminisce on the good times right now and one of those times was when Todd drew me his first picture at preschool and we hung it up on the refrigerator. It wasn't long and the whole fridge was of pictures and coloring book pages. It was at that point when we couldn't fit anything else on the door we decided to start a tradition called "Todd's box." Todd's box is a simple cardboard box and sits up in my bedroom closet. Every piece of paper that Todd brought home over the years is pressed down into that box. Not just his artwork, but homework assignments, report cards and everything else including Father Day cards and letters he wrote me.

I think after this is all over and Todd's out of the hospital we should take out Todd's box and take a look at it. It might be interesting to see some of the stuff that's in it.

This day seemed to take forever. Belinda's family had convinced her she needed to get some sleep in her own bed. Linda and I promised to call her if anything happened during the night. She didn't leave until seven o'clock and it wasn't two hours later a nurse came into the waiting room wanting to speak to me. She said Todd's condition didn't seem to be improving and the neurosurgeon wants to insert a stint in his head to relieve the pressure on his brain. They were taking him into surgery right now.

My understanding of the procedure went like this. The doctor would drill a hole into the skull and insert a tube. They would then drain off the fluid that was building up in the skull and hopefully remove some of the pressure off the brain.

I called Belinda and she immediately returned to the hospital. I can't tell you how long the surgery took, but it seemed like an eternity. A nurse stopped by and told us Todd has returned to his room and the doctor would be with us shortly.

The surgeon came in a few minutes later and had a very somber look on his face. His first words, and I'll never forget them were I'm afraid that Todd's condition is now dire. Those words just hit me like a ton a bricks and it must have hit Belinda that way too. We both broke down into tears. It finally struck us; we could be losing our son forever.

I drifted in and out of sleep that night. Linda was by my side and I could tell she too was having a difficult night. Here I was worrying if my son would ever come out of this chemically induced coma, yet I couldn't stop thinking about how much fun Todd and I had while he was growing up.

Todd started to play his two years in the peewees Little League at age six. It was a blast watching these six and seven year olds trying to learn the basics of baseball. The kids would hit the ball and instead of running to first base they would run towards third. Some would hit the ball and then chase after the ball. Then there were the boys who where no matter how many times I tried to explain, never could understand where to throw the ball. They always managed to throw it to the pitcher or the catcher.

I would have to classify Todd as a little above average baseball player. I really think he could have been an excellent player, but he lacked self-confidence. I can remember when he was in the last year of pony league, the 12 &13 years olds; he played most of the time in the outfield. I know this may sound like a disgruntled parent, but I definitely felt Todd wasn't given a fair chance to show his "stuff." When the coaches asked who wanted to try out for pitcher, Todd had said yes but he was never given the opportunity to show what he could do. One of the kids on the team was very good and I know Todd couldn't compete with him, but he was every bit as good as some of the others who got to play at the pitching position.

I can recall the last game of that season; Todd's team was getting killed early on in the game. The best pitcher on the team had used up all of his eligible pitching innings in the previous game. The coaches had gone through the rest of their pitchers and knew the game was lost. So just for fun they asked all the boys if any of them wanted to try and pitch. Todd spoke up and said he did. He struck out the first batter; the second batter hit a ground ball and was thrown out at first, and the third he struck out. After the game the coaches asked Todd where he had been all season.

Baseball wasn't the only team sport Todd was fairly good at. His first endeavor into team sports was a YMCA soccer team. I can't tell you if he was good at that or not. I think he was only five years old and all the kids at that age just ran around kicking the ball all over the place. I do remember it being a lot of fun to watch. Todd also played some YMCA basketball at a fairly early age.

Basketball was Todd's favorite sport and he played it all the way through grade school and CYO (Catholic Youth Organization) ball through high school. He again wasn't a great player, but he really enjoyed playing. I really think he could have been one of the better players if it wasn't again for his lack of confidence and having someone to teach and really work with him. Basketball was never my best sport and I lacked the knowledge to coach him properly. Football had always been my favorite sport, but unfortunately Todd didn't have the desire for it. He loved to watch it, but he just didn't have the killer instinct to excel in it.

I remembered when Todd decided he wanted to play football one year in grade school and I could tell his heart wasn't in it. His mother told me later that the only reason he went out was because he knew I liked football. I told him after one of his games that he shouldn't play on my account. We made an agreement that he honors our rule about playing until the end of the season, but he didn't have to go out again after that.

Todd's only other attempt at a sport was his freshman year at Roncalli High School. He went out for the cross-country team and I don't think anyone would argue, including Todd, that it was his worst athletic endeavor.

I really don't know why he went out for cross-country in the first place. Someone must have talked him into trying out. Whoever it was must have thought that since he had such long legs, he was a natural long distance runner. I can't tell you how far off that assumption may have been. I personally don't know much about the rules of cross-country, but I do know when you come in running about five to ten minutes after everyone else, it can't be a good thing. It was easy to see why Todd was terrible at running. Instead of taking long strides, Todd would place one foot down and the other would come pretty much right beside the other. It was a wonder he got anywhere at all. I told him, his mother told him, and I'm sure the coach and his teammates must have told him to stretch out his stride, but for some reason he just couldn't do it.

Todd and I were really close, especially those early years. Once when Todd was only about five or six years old we attended a figure eight car race with a neighbor and her children. One of the neighbor's kids was Todd's age and they sat several rows down from us. The stands were sparsely filled with people and there was no one sitting between us. One of the neighbor's kids was around two years old and sat on my lap. I was playing with him and I noticed Todd kept looking back at me with a worried look. It wasn't long before he was sitting right next to me with his arm around my back. My neighbor and I looked at each other smiling, knowing that Todd was jealous of the attention I was giving her son.

That evening I had a talk with Todd and I told him that I loved him more than anyone else. I also told him for the first time what became a regular catch phrase for the both of us, "You're my best buddy, always was and always will be."

CHAPTER 8

The morning of day seven finally came after a very restless night. The monitor beside Todd's bed read fourteen, which one of the nurses said was down from last night. I believe it was around 8:00 AM a nurse came into the waiting room and addressed all of the people in the room. She told us we were all welcome to attend a meeting at 10:00 AM in another waiting room. She said a couple of nurses would be there to explain to us what was going on with our respective family members and answer any questions we may have. They said it was optional for anyone who wanted to attend, but let them know in advance so they could bring the patient's charts and records.

Linda asked me if I would I mind if she ran down to check on her mother. She said, "She would be back in time for the ten o'clock meeting. I told her I'd walk her to the car, because I needed to take another walk.

I kissed Linda at the car and watched her pull out of the parking garage. I took the tunnel back to the lobby and headed out the front entrance of the hospital. It was strange that I thought about smoking a cigarette since I hadn't had a cigarette for over fifteen years. In fact I couldn't even remember when it was I last had the desire to have one.

I started smoking cigarettes with a few of my classmates when I was only twelve or thirteen years old. My parents didn't smoke, but my friend's parents did and we started by rifling a few cigarettes at a time from their open packs. By the time I was thirty I was up to three packs a day. All the time I smoked I can remember only once trying to quit. During my basic training at Fort Dix, New Jersey I caught the flu. The Army didn't mess around back then and as soon I was diagnosed they sent me directly to the hospital. I was immediately placed in quarantine so I wouldn't infect any of the other troops.

Sometime during the five days I spent in the hospital, I decided that since I did without a cigarette all that time I was going to quit for good. I can remember after my release it was about a two-mile walk from the hospital to my barracks. My old pack of Winston's was still in my shirt pocket and just two blocks away from the hospital I lit up my first cigarette. I coughed and gagged and immediately put it out. Good, I thought, never again. By the time I arrived at the barracks I had smoked two more cigarettes.

It was Todd who finally convinced me to quit smoking. I picked him up from day care on a Friday and he told me in a very adult tone that he wanted to talk to me about something. He said they had learned today about how bad cigarettes are. Todd emphatically told me that he didn't want me to die. I told Todd I couldn't promise him, but I would try to quit.

That was the first time I had a real desire to quit smoking. I gave up cigarettes not only because I didn't want to worry Todd about me dying. I also knew I had to set a good example. How could I teach my son right or wrong when I was doing something that terribly wrong?

That Saturday I had a whole pack of cigarettes left and I thought I'd smoke this last pack today and quit tomorrow. That night around six o'clock I had three cigarettes left and I decided to crumple up the pack and through it away. Until today I never looked back.

The real irony of this story is Todd started smoking at age fifteen.

I can't remember who all attended the meeting with Belinda, Linda, and I that morning. I do remember that only one other patient's family showed up.

Two of the intensive care unit's nurses greeted us at the door and asked us the name of the patient we wished to receive information on. A hospital staff member went to retrieve the charts of both Todd and the other patient. The nurses gave a brief introduction regarding the purpose of the meeting. They told us that both patients were being treated for head injuries due to blunt force accidents and explained a little more about their treatment. Immediately after their initial comments we were allowed to ask questions.

The other family asked a question about their family member; the nurses sounded very reassuring and went into great detail. When they answered questions about Todd the nurses seem to me to be very evasive in their answers. They never made eye contact and the answers were very brief. Often they would say that we should maybe talk to Todd's physician. When we told them we didn't even know the physician in charge of Todd's case, they gave us his name and said we should make an appointment. Immediately after the meeting, Belinda called and made an appointment for the following morning with the doctor.

I left the meeting very troubled. I went down stairs and started to take another walk around the hospital grounds. Linda had left again saying she was going to work or to go check on her mother; I can't remember which. She told me later, she really didn't have to do either, but she needed to get away from the hospital. I didn't realize how much pain she was in. Linda knew that I was overburdened with worry and didn't want to compound things by unloading on me. She really loved Todd and was grieving in the worst way. She, too, recognized Todd's lack of confidence and felt terribly sorry for him.

Todd's feelings of inferiority I believe contributed to his troubled teen years. I can't pinpoint one factor in Todd's life that made him feel that way, but I'm sure that his adoption played a part. Todd's mother and I never kept his adoption a secret from him. I sat him down at a very early age and told him how his mother and I wanted a child to love, but we couldn't have children of our own. I explained to him how we went to an adoption agency to help find us a baby. I then told Todd about a young lady who was going to have a baby and was worried that she couldn't take care of the baby once it arrived. She loved the baby very much and wanted to find a good home for it. She ended up at the same adoption agency and so everything worked out great. She found someone to raise and care for her baby and we found the most wonderful child to love.

I can remember only one time when Todd raised the question of his adoption. He must have been eleven years old when he asked me if I would help him find his birth mother and father. He said he'd asked his mom and she gave him a flat out "no." I understood his curiosity and told him that I would be very glad to help him in any way I can, but I asked him to wait a few years. He said okay and never again raised the question.

When Todd was around fourteen or fifteen I gave him the following poem I wrote about his being adopted. I can tell you that unless you're an adoptive parent you will never be able to understand this fully.

MY ADOPTED CHILD

When first they told me I'd have not child of my own,
Disappointment so painful never had I known.
The options they gave me were a limited few,
So adoption was the route, I decided to pursue

The testing and home studies, a long two-year wait,
Yet all worth the trouble for the happiness so great.
To those who may wonder or to question are prone,
This child without doubt is the same as my own.
I want to assure you, this child is loved well,

And further I promise no way will that fail.
I thank the young mother for the choice that she made,
And the Almighty in heaven for the child that He gave.

The poem I wrote meant a lot to Todd, because he had it framed and displayed it proudly on the desk I made for him.

I could probably name a half dozen other reasons Todd felt a little estranged from his peers. He was an only child of divorced parents and attended a parochial school system. I know in grade school he and just one other kid in his class were from broken homes. I know this had to have an effect him, my wife Linda probably could explain it better than I could, for she too had been a product of that type of environment.

My second marriage to Becky, a stepfamily situation that lasted for three years, didn't help either. Todd was around eight or nine years old when Becky and I were married and it was probably the biggest mistake I ever made. Becky had two boys from a previous marriage both younger than Todd. We did have a few good moments especially some great camping trips including a week stay in the Great Smokey Mountains. Then again it was also during that marriage Todd and I experienced the worst vacation I ever had, which I've now come to refer to as the "Vacation from Hell."

Becky was an avid camper long before me. I had some camping experience both in the National Guard and with Todd's mother, but it wasn't my favorite way to vacation. When Becky and I first were married we did a lot of tent camping. Later Becky mentioned she would like to have a pop up tent camper and I was all for not having to sleep on the ground. After about a year of that we decided to move up to a travel trailer, so we bought a twenty-four foot camper, which of course was too big to pull with a our little Ford Escort.

We purchased a used Chevy passenger van with a V8, 350 horse engine to pull the travel trailer. I had the suspension strengthened by adding several springs, plus I added heavy-duty shocks. I found out that it still wasn't good enough and I needed to have a bigger and better transmission. I spent at least $600.00 for a rebuilt one to be installed.

We had our itinerary all planned out for an aggressive two-week vacation. We left on a Saturday and our first stop was Mt. Rogers in Virginia. It was located in an Appalachian Mountain national recreation area and was the highest point in that state.

In order to reach Mt. Rogers we had to travel through Kentucky on I 64 and into West Virginia where it and I-77 run together as a toll road. Just before we reached the toll road we stopped at a small pleasant restaurant to eat a late lunch.

I asked the kids if anyone needed to go to the bathroom before we left and all but the youngest stepchild decided to make a pit stop. We no more than got a block away from the toll roads ticket booth when my stepchild decided he had to go to the bathroom. I don't know how far we had to drive to the next exit, but I can remember the kid screaming like crazy that he had to go real bad.

Once we made the necessary stop we continued on to our first destination. We reached the base of the mountain and started up the steep looping two-lane road. When we had gone just few hundred yards up the incline I heard a loud grinding noise and the van began to shake. It gradually slowed to a crawl and there was no place to pull off the road. I had the accelerator peddle pushed all the way to the floor and all I could get out of it was five miles per hour. This did not sit well with miles of honking cars behind me by the time we reached the mountain's summit.

When we reached the campground I unhooked the trailer from the van and set the camper up. This wasn't an easy chore with all the leveling and hook ups. I decided to try the van without the burden of pulling the trailer. It took off real slow, and I could still hear a rattle below the floor of the cab. It finally picked speed once it ground through the lower gears of the transmission.

We went to the park office and called the closest town at the foot of the mountain with a repair shop. I believe it was "Gomer Pyle" who answered the phone or maybe his cousin Goober. They said they could probably fix the van, but it would take at least a week. I tried to give them a hard luck story about being stranded and having reservations in Florida, but he didn't waver. He said it would take at least five or six days just to get another rebuilt transmission.

I asked the park attendant what was the nearest big town and he said Bristol which was about fifty miles away via the state highway. I then asked how far it was if I took the interstate since I didn't want to do a lot of stopping or slowing down. He said I had to tack on another ten to twenty miles.

I called information to find a transmission repair shop in Bristol, Virginia. This time I received some better news. If I could get the van there Sunday and use their key drop they couldn't guarantee it, but would try everything possible to have it done Monday afternoon.

I told Becky there wasn't any sense for all of us to go to Bristol and she agreed. Todd wanted to stay with me and asked if he could come along. I agreed it was for the best and Todd and I headed to Bristol Sunday morning. The van took what seemed like forever to get up to a decent speed and every time we stopped or slowed down we had to start all over again. When we got to the Interstate the van cruised along around sixty miles per hour which was great considering the circumstances.

We found the transmission shop without a problem and dropped off the van. We were fortunate that it was within walking distance of a fairly nice hotel. Todd and I spent the night and even caught a movie at a nearby theater complex. I can honestly say that time I spent with Todd alone was the best part of that trip. The next day the garage was able to finish the job of fixing the transmission by noon, which was great, except he charged us another five hundred dollars. When I got home I complained to the transmission shop that installed the rebuilt transmission in the van. They said there wasn't anything they could do; the transmission was under warranty only if they did the work and sure enough that's what the contract said.

Todd and I drove back to the campground and had the privilege of spending one afternoon at our first destination before we needed to get back on the road and head to Florida. We traveled without incident until we stopped for gas at a service station just outside of Jacksonville, Fl. This was at a time when full service stations were still abundant and I sat in the van as the attendant filled the gas tank. I looked out my side mirror and noticed the attendant was fooling with the Indianapolis Colts spare tire cover on the rear of the van. I stepped out from the vehicle and asked him what he was doing. He said the cover looked loose to him and was just checking it.

I checked the cover myself and it seemed pretty secure to me and I told him not to worry about it. The attendant then proceeded to tell me that my shocks on the van looked bad and they needed to be replaced right away. I told him that there wasn't anything wrong with the shocks they were brand new as was the rest of the suspension. I went back to the van and sat there waiting for him to finish filling the tank. A second attendant walked up and started carrying on a conversation with the first, blocking my view of the one filling up the tank.

I paid the man for the gas and headed to our next destination, which was a campground in Kissimmee, a tourist town just outside of Orlando and Walt Disney World. I stopped again for gas just before we reached the campground. It only got around ten miles a gallon regularly and less than that when pulling the trailer. I got out to pump the gas myself when I got to the back of the van I couldn't believe my eyes. My $50.00 Indianapolis Colts wheel cover was missing.

We arrived at the campground early in the evening and as I pulled into the gate I heard a pop and the trailer seemed to tilt a little to the passenger side. I already had guessed what the problem was when I checked and found a flat tire on one of the trailers outside dual wheels.

I knew it was too late to search for a repair shop and the trailer was fine as long as the inside tire stayed healthy. We went to the trailer park office and checked in. We were told where to park our trailer and immediately started the process of setting up and leveling the trailer.

We were eating a late supper outside when a neighbor lady, who I thought was coming over to greet us, walked right up to me. I didn't have even time to say good evening before the lady started screaming, "One of your boys just walked across our campsite. This isn't the family site area, what are you doing setting up here?"

I calmly told the lady that this is where the office told us to set up. She said she was going to complain to the office. I said fine.

We let our dog Frodo out of the trailer and chained him up right next to where we were sitting. All of a sudden a small dog started barking like crazy from inside the neighbor's trailer. Frodo not to be outdone started barking back. The same old grumpy lady came running outside and right up to me yelling that I was going to have to move. I said, "Excuse me?" She screamed your dog is bothering my dog. By this time my normally patient demeanor was running a bit thin. I turned to Becky and said I'm not putting up with this for a whole week and walked over to the park office.

I explained to the night manager what had transpired. She told me there wasn't a designated family area in the park and told me the "old bat" didn't know what she was talking about. She offered us a prime location in the park close to the playground and swimming pool and I took her up on the offer. She also said she was going to talk to the lady tomorrow and set her straight.

I went back to the campsite and told Becky to pack up, we were moving. She started to argue that we shouldn't move, but I was able to convince her it would be a better place for us as a family. We packed up everything hitched up the trailer and drove a couple a blocks over to the new location where we went through the whole setting up process all over again. I remember when we left the old location I noticed a man who I'm assuming was the husband of the tyrannical old lady, standing behind the screen door of the trailer next door. It was almost as if he was cowering and embarrassed by his wife's actions and I almost felt sorry for him. At least we could pick up and leave; he was still stuck with the old Witch from the West.

The next morning I jacked up the trailer and removed the tire and discovered a large split that I knew couldn't be patched. I went to two service stations where the attendants said they couldn't replace the tire. On my third try the mechanic said he could fix it for two hundred and forty dollars. I asked him why it would cost that much money to change a tire. He said it took a special tool to remove and place the new tire on the rim. I told him I didn't want to buy the tool so I went to another place, which cut a hundred dollars off the previous station's price. I still thought that to be a bit pricey and went to a RV dealership down the road, which fortunately had a repair shop too. The service manager there did verify that it did take a special tool to change a trailer tire, but he was only going to charge seventy dollars including the tire. He also told me that the other stations that I visited would have sent the tire to his service department to have it repaired, because they didn't even have the tool.

I replaced the tire when I got back to the campground and found the boys and Becky swimming in the park's pool. It being a little late I decided we shouldn't hit the amusement parks until the next day so I let the boys swim.

I can remember the rest of the day being quite pleasant. The boys had made friends with the family a few spaces down from us and were having a good time. That evening we had roasted hot dogs on the open campfire and we fed the tame gray squirrels that came close to our picnic table begging for a handout.

That night the boys were tired and went to bed early. Becky and I sat up watching television when Todd became the focus of our entertainment. Ever since I can remember Todd was an occasional sleep talker and sometimes a sleepwalker.

Often Todd would visit my bedroom in the middle of the night and just carry on a sometimes-coherent conversation. He'd talk about baseball or school and a lot of times I would find out things by asking him more questions. Of course there were other times where he wouldn't make any sense at all.

The night in the camper was one of those nights where he was somewhat coherent, but not completely. He started out by calling me. "Dad what time is it tomorrow?" I answered, "what do you mean what time is it tomorrow? Do you want to know what day it is?"

There would be some silence and then he would say something else, but the highlight of the conversation came when he sat up in his bed._The upper bunk where Todd preferred to sleep was only two feet from the ceiling of the trailer.

When Todd sat up and started to talk he hit his head on the ceiling and just said, "Oh!" and laid right back down to sleep. Becky and I just laughed after I went back to see if he was all right.

The next day the nightmare of the trip started up again. The focal point of our trip was to take the boys to Disneyworld. Todd had been there before, but this was the first time Becky's two boys had been to the park. We arrived at the park a few minutes before the gates opened. We weren't there for an hour, before the boys started to complain, it's too hot, I don't want to walk, I don't want to stand in line, I want to go swimming back at the trailer park.

Becky started to cater to the boys telling me we should consider leaving the park and let the boys go swimming. I told her that we just paid a small fortune to get into the gate and this was the point of coming here in the first place. I told her the boys could go swimming any time the wanted at her parent's swimming pool at home; I didn't drive over nine hundred miles just so the boys could go swimming.

An hour later I couldn't put up with the fussing any longer and decided to pack it in. The boys weren't having any fun and they made sure that Becky and I weren't going to enjoy the experience either. We got to the campground and even before I opened the air-conditioned trailer door I could smell an offensive order. Our dog Frodo had gotten sick in the trailer and believe me he was sick. He had thrown up and had diarrhea from one end of the trailer to the other. It wasn't bad enough on the floor but he had also gone on every lower bed in the trailer.

Let me tell you that I've got a pretty strong stomach with one major exception and that's the sight and smell of vomit. Todd has known for years that when he was sick he had to make it to the bathroom, because he was on his own when cleaning up the mess if he missed.

Becky and I spent the rest of the day cleaning out the trailer and doing all the bedding at the campgrounds laundry room. It wasn't until we got the trailer completely back together again when Becky noticed I was red and tired looking.

She asked me if I was all right and all I could say was I felt like Chevy Chase from his Vacation movies.

Becky laughed and sighed with relief. Her first husband, the boy's father, she said would have blown a gasket by now. She was glad I had a much calmer demeanor.

The initial plan for the trip was to stop at the Smoky Mountains for a couple of days on the way back home. I had made a decision earlier in the week to cancel our reservation at the campground in Pigeon Forge, Tennessee. There were two reasons for that decision; first I was sick and tired of this so-called vacation. Secondly, I didn't want to take a chance of driving through the mountains again while pulling the trailer. So instead, of stopping in the Smokey's or taking a direct route home, I decided to take a long route around the lower foothills of the mountains. That was definitely one of those trips where I needed a vacation to recover from the vacation. We decided after that vacation experience to find a nice private campground and take that big trailer and park it.

Becky and my marriage should have never happened. We had problems almost from the start in which I will not go into the details. Let's just say we were completely different people. I will say the step-family situation did play a big part in the marriages demise.

Prior to our marriage I had insisted that Becky understood that Todd was to be considered a full member of our family. Though she readily agreed with me, it wasn't six months after we were married she told me she no longer felt that way. She felt her kids deserved more than Todd did because they were living with us all of the time. Though I set her straight on the subject, there was always a double standard on her part regarding the boys. To make a long story short I will just say that when I told Todd that Becky and I were getting divorced he gave out a loud happy scream yelling, "YES!"

To get back to some of Todd's problems, it's strange how the pattern emerges with some people's inferiority complex. In some cases that person withdraws further into a shell. In Todd's case he tried so hard to be noticed. When Todd was little, he wanted so much to please everyone, especially his mother and I. As he got older he wanted to be accepted by his friends, but sometimes his forwardness would target him with teasing from other kids. This of course only compounded his already bruised ego.

Todd then decided to go a different route, one that probably led him to where he is today.

CHAPTER 9

The rest of the day was uneventful at the hospital. I can't remember if Linda and I went home to sleep that night or not. I can remember going with Todd's mother to the doctor's office the next morning, which was located in another wing of the hospital.

Doctor Rogers was a highly respected brain surgeon and didn't mince any words when we sat down to speak with him. He started the conversation with the first question. What exactly do you know about Todd's condition? We told him what we knew, that Todd was still in critical condition and some details of his injury. So the doctor asked what else we wanted to know. I don't think he meant it to sound as abrupt as it came out, but it sounded like "okay, you have the facts, what do you want from me."

Belinda asked the doctor, just what he thought were Todd's chances of recovery. The doctor never spoke Todd's name, but started to talk about head injuries in general. He said, " medical science has advanced rapidly over the past ten years and head trauma patients now have a greater than ever chance of survival." "There is a draw back," he said, "Patients survive but most are impaired in some way or another. He went on to tell us that we should expect a long rehabilitation and a strong possibility of permanent damage.

Belinda and I never even thought that far ahead. We both were still looking for some assurance that he was going to live. The doctor remained uncommitted about that and said only time will tell.

Belinda and I left the doctor's office neither more nor less encouraged. I went back to the waiting room and informed Linda what had transpired. She asked if I would be alright if she went to the office to work for a little bit. I said, she might as well go since nothing was going on here. Linda asked me if I should get away from here for a while and go back to work until something develops. It was a similar question the Police Department's Chaplain asked me earlier this week. He said, "Is this the place I need to be right now." I gave Linda the same answer as I gave the chaplain, until I know Todd's out of the woods or least shows some sign of recovery this is where I *have* to be.

I walked Linda out to the car in the hospital garage and from there I proceeded to take yet another one of my walks. I started reflecting back to a less than pleasant phone call I had received from Todd when he was around fifteen years old. He called to let me know that he had tried marijuana at a friend's house that day. I was just ready to lay into him with both barrels when he told me not to worry, that he didn't like it and would never try it again. I still went off on him, telling him how stupid it was to even try it and asked if he had told his mother. He said, he did and that she was alright with it as long as I didn't do it again.

Soon after that it seemed Todd started arguing more and more with his mother. For years Todd had tried to pit his mother and me against each other, whenever he didn't get his way. We didn't fall for this ploy and would always back each other up. Belinda and I argued a lot about medical bills and other things, but we would never allow Todd to play us to his advantage.

Todd started to call me on a regular basis, begging me to pick him up, saying he wanted to live with me. It was something I always wanted, but I knew it couldn't be on his terms. It had to be a mutual agreement on his, mine, and his mother's part. I would listen to what he had to say, but never contradict Belinda. Sometimes Todd would complain about how unfair his mother was and she really didn't want him there. As time wore on things got worse and Belinda would often ask me to come over and discuss some of the problems she was having. We would then have another talk with Todd to try to bring him under control. I even tried to defuse things when Todd would come over to my house telling him he needed to quit arguing with his mother.

Todd's temper kept getting worse as time wore on. His mother finally gave up and told Todd he could come live with me. Todd was overjoyed and so was I, but before long he started to act up at my house too.

We would argue continuously over how he dressed and about the music he was listening to and playing loudly. He wore the baggy pants way below his waist imitating the rap singers and gang bangers of the day. I know that sounds prudish but that's not the case. My parents never yelled at me or my brother or sisters for listening to rock and roll music, as some of the parents of our generation did. I'll tell you the truth; I couldn't care less if Todd wanted to listen to rap style music, even if I didn't care for the music myself. It was the content of the music that I couldn't condone. The music he preferred had extremely violent overtones, foul language, and sexually explicit lyrics and I wouldn't put up with it.

Many evenings I'd come home from work and he'd have the music volume blaring so loud that I could hear it several houses down the street. I'd come in the door screaming at the top of my lungs telling him to turn it off.

Things came to a head one-day when I woke up in the morning and Todd wasn't there. On his bed he had left the following note.

Dad,

I am going away for a while. Today some kid that I know pulled a gun on me and put it to my head, he took my money and my hat. I love you but this kid threatened me and he knows where I live and where I work. He said he would kill me the next time he saw me. I know you'll be mad but I'll be back.

PS. I'm scared he has killed people. I'll be back. Trust me. Talk to my mom and tell her I really love her.

Your Son, Todd

I was really upset after reading the letter and started to call some of the officers I worked with. They said they would have someone from the Marion County Sheriff's Department give me a call. I called my then girlfriend Linda and she came over to help.

A lady from the sheriff's department called me within a half-hour of my notifying the department. She asked me the make of Todd's car and several other questions regarding his description. She said she'd have the officers keep a look out for him and would check out all the teenage hangouts.

I called everyone I could think of, including his friend Jeff, who I just happened to have a phone number to. He said, he hadn't heard from Todd and said he's been hanging around a couple of kids from a different neighborhood, who nobody really liked. I told him that if Todd should contact him to have him give me a call immediately. After a long grueling day it was around seven in the evening and Todd finally called.

He said he and a couple of his buddies were heading to Florida and were calling from Cave City, Kentucky. He said one of the guys knew someone in Tampa that would give them a job and a place to stay. Todd told me he had spoke to his friend Danny and was told I wanted to speak to him. I proceeded to tell him, I just wanted to know what was going on.

Todd told me the letter wasn't completely true. A kid did threaten him, but not with a gun. He told me that he didn't feel like I wanted him there anymore and he wasn't ever coming back. I could tell by the sound of his voice that he was really scared, but trying to act tough.

We spoke for some time and I finally convinced him that he needed to come home so we could talk about it. He said, he couldn't come home right away, that he had promised to take these guys down to Florida. Supposedly, one of the boys was in trouble with the law. He was on probation and one of the conditions of his probation was he couldn't leave Marion county.

I asked Todd if I could to talk to his friends and they were just as much wanting to be talked into coming back home as Todd.

Things only got worse after that incident. We had just moved into a house after living in an apartment for the last three years. His mother and I received a phone call from the Beech Grove police department and we were to meet with an officer there. They wanted Todd to come too.

We arrived at the appointed time and were escorted back to Officer Johnson's desk. He told us that the apartment complex Todd and I used to live at had requested that Todd no longer come on the premises. The officer explained that several of the boys were playing basketball at the apartment complex and Todd was identified as hanging on the rim and bent it down.

Todd vehemently denied having done it. He said there were lots of guys playing and all of them were hanging on the rim. The officer said that he had talked to some of the other boys and though he admitted that there were other boys involved with the damage, Todd had been identified as the main culprit.

Todd finally admitted his part in the bent rim, but again said he wasn't the only one. I asked if the apartment complex wanted compensation for the rim and the officer said no. They just asked that Todd not come back on the property. We all agreed.

Within a week, Todd was caught by the same officer at the apartment complex. He was charged with trespassing which of course Todd said wasn't his fault. He said, he thought he just couldn't play basketball there anymore and thought it was alright to visit his friends.

I went to court with him a couple of weeks later and the judge gave Todd a big lecture on trespassing and said if he was caught again that he would end up in jail. Two weeks later Todd was once again caught over at Willow Glen.

This time the Judge still didn't throw Todd in jail, but charged him with a misdemeanor and gave him a year's probation.

Todd soon started to skip school and I would catch him sneaking out in the middle of the night. He started to hang around a bunch of kids that soon turned into a regular south side gang. These kids were a mixture of want-a-be gang members, with a couple of true punks heading them up. Barry, the leader of this gang, was well known by the local police. I overheard a girl once asking Todd why he did everything Barry asked him to do. Todd told her that he would die for Barry.

In February of Todd's senior year at high school, I got a phone call from the Dean. He said, " Todd was in his office and he is having some problems at school. He also told me that Todd doesn't want to go to Roncalli High School anymore and he wanted to go to Franklin Township public school. My first thought was how stupid this whole conversation was, since Todd only had four more months of school left. All he had to do was stay in school till the end of the semester and he could have graduated from one of the leading high schools in the state. I told the Dean that I didn't think Todd should leave Roncalli that his tuition is paid for the year and I thought he should finish the term. Then I started to get a little upset with the Dean when he started to argue with me on the phone with Todd sitting right next to him.

He said he felt since Todd really didn't want to be at Roncalli that he should at least be able to check out Franklin Central High School. He said it was better if he did that rather than fail his senior year. I continued to argue more, but finally relented to allow Todd to check out the other high school. When Todd came home I wasn't in a very good mood. I had called his mother and she wasn't very happy with the situation either. We both tried to talk some sense into his head, but he insisted on looking into the other school, with the ammunition of the Dean's backing.

Todd said the kids at Roncalli all made fun of him and nobody liked him there; he went on to say he had friends at the other school. Belinda and I knew too that there was another motive for him to go to the other school. Todd had almost all the credits he needed to graduate from Franklin Central High School and would only have to take one or two classes. At Roncalli, he would have at least four more classes to graduate.

Belinda and I relented and allowed him to check out Franklin Central and of course he was enthusiastic when he got back from his initial meeting with the staff.

I had talked to Belinda while Todd was gone and we decided to allow him to finish school there if he agreed to quit skipping school and graduate.

Todd agreed to the terms we laid out, but it wasn't but a few weeks later, I caught him skipping school again. He did squeak by his last semester though and graduated with the rest of the Franklin Central class of 1997.

Todd's grandfather, Belinda, and I attended his graduation and were extremely proud. I can also tell you for a guy who often said he couldn't care less about graduating he was very happy he had. He often told me in the following years that he was glad I'd made him stick it out.

Todd had tried several part time jobs while in high school. Two of the neighborhood grocery stores had given him a try. He started out like a bang at the first place and the manager had complimented him often. He then started to miss work occasionally and he was soon let go. He immediately went to work for the other store and didn't even last a month. The story I got was he was out talking to his buddies in the parking lot and sometimes in the store. The store manager had warned him several times and Todd got mouthy with him. Todd still being on new hire probation was quickly dismissed.

Todd's obvious behavior showed all the signs of alcohol and drug abuse. I would question him often and tried about everything I could to get him into counseling. I even talked to counselors at our employee wellness program, but was told there was little they could do if Todd wasn't willing to come in and talk to them.

Todd had turned eighteen just prior to graduating high school. I told him he needed to find a job right away, because he was going to have to pay for his room and board. His first reaction was one of indignation and he threatened to run away.

I laughed and said there's the front door. I told him he was eighteen and if he wanted to leave there wasn't anything I could do about it, but if you want to stay here you'll have to find a job.

He claimed he couldn't find a job, because he didn't have a car after wrecking two previous vehicles. I told him, "Don't even think about me buying you a car."

Todd's mother had given him her old Escort when he turned sixteen and received his driver's license. Within a couple months he'd totaled the car while taking a curve too fast. His mother had allowed him to work at the gift shop she managed and soon he was able to buy another Escort and it too had met the fate of the first within a few months. Todd and his mother couldn't get along at home; you can only imagine the fights they got into at work.

Todd finally found a job at the ten-minute oil change place close the house. There seemed to be a few months of sobriety at that point and the old Todd had emerged and it was a great time for the both of us.

CHAPTER 10

I tried not to feel discouraged about the news regarding Todd possibly being severely handicapped if he survives. Instead I tried to take comfort in what he said regarding the vast improvement in survival rates with head trauma patients in recent years.

I went back to Todd's bedside several times that day praying and talking to him. I was really getting worried now, because his brain pressure monitor seemed to be all over the place. One hour it would be up to twenty-four and then back to sixteen and then back up again.

A nurse came out and told us that they were having a difficult time controlling his brain pressure with the medication.

That night wasn't a very restful one for any of us. My mind kept churning over the past few years as I tried to think if there was something I could have done to prevent all of this. It would seem I'd be used to this kind of situation where Todd was concerned. The last five years had been nothing but one troubling predicament after another.

I naively thought Todd had turned himself around once he started working at the Quick Lube place down the street from where we lived. He was real enthusiastic about the job, explaining the long-range training program that could lead him into a management position one day. He had a few new friends and the bosses seemed to like him.

Todd's personality had totally changed and had reverted back to the Todd I used to know several years ago. We went on a couple short day trips together with some of my friends and their sons. I can remember all of us going to Paramount's Kings Island amusement park in Cincinnati and having a ball. On another trip we went to a cave in southern Indiana; afterwards we went over to my favorite eating spot, the Amish Gastauf Restaurant in Montgomery, Indiana.

It was really nice having the old Todd back, but unfortunately things started to reverse themselves. Todd became moody and complained that he had a new boss at work who didn't like him. He tried going to the shop where his old boss was transferred to, but he kept missing days and soon was released.

We started to argue again mostly about him finding a job. He would tell me he had applied at some places within walking distance, but couldn't find anything. His Grandfather bought him another Escort and he was quickly running out of excuses not to be working.

Todd's attitude got worse over the next few months and his friends seemed to get seedier. I'd come home from work and hear music blaring throughout the neighborhood. When I burst into the house yelling, five or six of his friends would file out. I finally had to forbid him to have anyone in the house while I was gone.

One day I gave Todd an ultimatum. He had one month to find a job or he was out the door. I don't think it registered with him, because I saw him make no effort at all to look. I reminded him about every other day, but he would just grunt and say okay, I heard you. Finally the last day came and I told him to pack his bags and leave. Todd threw a fit and acted like he couldn't believe that I would throw him out. I asked him if he ever remembered me telling him something and not following through on it. I can remember once when he and his stepbrother were fighting in the back seat of the car on a trip to Florida. I warned them once to knock it off, they kept it up and I warned them again, this time I said they were going to be spanked if they didn't quit. They were quiet for five minutes and then back at again. I said that was it and they were going to be spanked at the next stop. We drove at least a hundred miles, before we stopped for lunch. The boys had been behaving since my last threat, but Todd should have already known I never threaten punishment and then not carry it out. I opened the back door of the car and as Todd and his stepbrother got out I smacked them both on the bottom. I never will forget the surprised look on their faces.

I went to work the morning after telling Todd he had to be gone by the time I got home. That evening when I arrived home Todd had cleaned everything out of his room, with one exception. The poem I had written about his adoption was prominently displayed on his bookshelf. It was Todd's way of letting me know he didn't think I meant what I wrote and I was being unfair.

For two weeks after that I had noticed that Todd was somehow getting into the house. Towels were wet, food was missing, and there would be a big imprint on my bed where he must have stretched out during the day. I put a bar in his bedroom window, because I knew he would come in that way when he lost his keys. The house was a tri-level and all the bedrooms were upstairs. Todd was over six foot three by then and could easily reach up and climb in.

I was really getting some bad reports on some of Todd's activities. My sister told me that Todd and one of his friends were caught in my Dad's back yard. Dad had pulled up into the drive and Todd told him that he was waiting for him because he noticed the back door window was broken. My sister confided in me later that Dad at eighty-two years old was afraid of Todd. I didn't blame him; we both loved Todd, but neither of us was sure what Todd was capable of.

Todd was still getting into the house somehow and I finally figured it out. I came home and noticed the sliding glass door to the back yard was unlocked when I'm sure I had locked it. I found out you could lift up on the door and slide it over the lock mechanism. I placed a bar in the tracks of the door so Todd could no longer get in that way either.

The very next morning after I had fixed the doors in the back, I had noticed Todd's car parked on the side of the house. We lived on a corner and he was waiting for me to go to work so he could break in again. I pulled up to the car and he had the seat reclined back and he was sleeping soundly. His car was packed full of his possessions. I had thought possibly one of his buddies had taken him in, but obviously that wasn't the case. I felt really bad; here was the child I loved and cared for, living out of his car.

I tapped on his car window and asked him to come inside so we could talk. He threw a fit and said, he was done talking to me and he was just fine. He didn't need anyone and it didn't matter anymore anyway, because he was probably going to jail. I asked him what he was talking about and he said some of his buddies and he had broken into some cars in Plainfield and had stolen some car stereos. The police had a warrant out for his arrest.

I asked him how he knew there was a warrant out and he said one of his friends had already been arrested. The kid's parents had told one of Todd's friends that the police were looking for Todd.

I begged him to come inside so we could discuss it further, but he continued to refuse. I told him I had barred the back door, so he couldn't get in that way anymore and if he wanted to take a shower he'd have to go in with me now. He told me to unlock the back door so he could get in later himself. I explained to him that I couldn't do that. I told him the best thing for him to do right now was to turn himself in and face the music. He turned on his car and sped off.

A few days later Todd called me from the lock up at the Marion County Jail. He told me the police had caught up with him at a friend's apartment. He asked if I could check on his car. The Beech Grove police had taken it along with all of his belongings. I asked Todd why they took his car and he said he didn't know. The police just told him to give them his car keys and he told them all his belongings were in it. Then one of the officers yelled to another, " Hey, we got all of Todd's stuff. "

I will admit I was a little worried what the police might find in Todd's car. I also was concerned with the manner it was impounded. Todd believed and related to me that the Beech Grove police were always trying to hassle him and his buddies. They were always pulling him over for some minor traffic violation such as seat belt checks even when he had his seat belt on. I have such high respect for the police officers I work with, that I knew they were just trying to keep a tab on Todd and his gang. I would never allow Todd to believe I'd take his side over the police. This time though I felt the Beech Grove police may have overstepped their bounds.

Beech Grove is a small town totally encompassed by the city of Indianapolis with a population of less than twenty thousand. It was the town I grew up in and never strayed too far from its location on the south side of Indy. When I was younger the town was quiet and all the Main Street shops closed no later than six o'clock every day.

I had several friends who had regular newspaper routes and whenever any of them had to miss a day, I was the first one they called. In fact, the man who ran the paper distribution station in town got to know me so well, he put me on a call list if one of his carriers didn't show up. I'm telling this story, just let you know I was very familiar with every inch of the town and though it's grown slightly there isn't much that I didn't know about the area.

"The Grove" as the town's people refer to the community hasn't changed a great deal over the years. Crime may have increased some, but a major case such as a murder would still make the headlines. The old section of town seems to have its share of thefts and reportedly there have been some small groups of teenage gangs in the area. When I was growing up you'd rarely see one of the town's four police cars patrolling the streets. Today it's very rare I don't see one the town's several police cars when I go visit dad who still lives in the house where we grew up.

Officer Johnson was the only one I currently knew by name on the Beech Grove police department. I only knew him because of Todd's previous misadventures. It was Johnson who nailed Todd on the trespassing charges and it was him who seemed to be keeping the closest tabs on Todd's activities.

When Todd was arrested for the outstanding warrant, it was Officer Johnson who made the arrest and he was also the one who took Todd's car keys. What bothered me about this scenario was the arrest was made outside of the Beech Grove's jurisdiction and secondly I couldn't understand why the officer had taken his car.

I called Officer Johnson the next day to find out which impound lot had Todd's car. He said, he hadn't taken it to an impound lot and that Todd's car was at the Beech Grove police station where he planned to search through it today. I then asked him why he had taken Todd's car and he said he was looking for evidence.

I asked if he had Todd's permission to search the car or did he have a search warrant? He said, since Todd had a warrant out on him he didn't need one.

I told him, I'd have to consult an attorney, but I think he was way off base. Todd's car was parked in a parking lot of an apartment complex where he had been invited by one the residents; the officer didn't have the right to take the car.

At that point the conversation got a little ugly. Officer Johnson shouted a few obscenities. He ended by saying he didn't care what I did, he had Todd's car and he was going through it. He then hung up on me.

Needless to say this really ticked me off. I won't defend Todd's actions and whatever punishment the court dealt out I would accept, as long as the outcome was done justly. I just couldn't allow this officer to railroad Todd with his personal vendetta. Yes, I know part of my anger was my parental protection kicking in, but there was more to it than that. Todd would often complain about something or someone being unfair. All I could say to him was life is unfair sometimes and he'd just have to accept it. Yet, this would be an injustice that could have been prevented, if the Officer would follow the proper procedures.

I called the Beech Grove police back immediately and asked to speak to Officer Johnson's supervisor. The lady who answered the phone said that his immediate supervisor, who wasn't in at the moment was the department's assistant chief. She said, she would leave a message for him to return my call.

It was probably better that I didn't' speak to the chief right away, because it gave me some time to cool off. When the chief called back I was very calm and told the story, as I knew it and I told him I didn't appreciate Johnson's attitude. The chief said he'd have to check into it and he'd get back to me the next day.

The next morning I received a call from the chief, and he told me I could pick up Todd's car in the police station parking lot. I asked him why the car taken in the first place and did they search it. He said, "the car hadn't been searched," and Officer Johnson took the car because he knew Todd's belongings were in it and he was looking out for Todd's interest.

That lie got me madder than ever. I asked the chief if that was the case, why didn't Officer Johnson tell me a completely different story? The chief said he didn't know what Johnson had told me, but it was okay and I could come and get the car.

At first I didn't know if Officer Johnson had lied to his supervisor or together they had conspired together to switch his story. After pressing a little further, I realized the latter was the case. The chief indicated at one point during our conversation, he didn't understand my objections; after all, Todd is a criminal.

I had my dad pick me up from home and drop me at the Beech Grove police department's parking lot. I could really tell the officers were looking out for Todd's belongings and his best interest. The car had sat out there all night with windows rolled down and the doors unlocked.

Side note on this story is when I got the car home I emptied it completely out, all I found were Todd's clothes, CD's, and baseball card collection.

I've always had and still have the greatest respect for the officers I work with.

Ninety-nine point nine percent of them are top of the line individuals. I have seen these men and women in action and I personally could never do what they do day in and day out. This may sound like a cliché but they are brave, caring, and dedicated to do their job of protecting law-biding citizens. The errant ones you read about in the paper or see on the news are in a very small minority.

The more I thought about Officer Johnson going out of his way to arrest Todd even outside his jurisdiction, I was glad he did it. I believe it was the best thing for Todd, because who knows how much more trouble he could get into. The police shouldn't have to do the job of the parents but in some cases when a child is totally out of hand their intervention should be appreciated and not maligned.

A few days after Todd's arrest, he was transferred from Marion County to the Hendricks County Jail where he was to await trial. He started to call every other night and I could tell the drugs were starting to wear off. His mother and I met to discuss what we should do. We decided to help him out by hiring a decent attorney. The price tag was high and I think Belinda would agree he wasn't worth the expense. I still believe Todd would have faired better with a court appointed attorney.

The Hendricks County Jail only allowed visitors one day a week for each of the cellblocks. This was due to staffing problems at the jail. Todd's visitation day was on Tuesdays and his mother and I decided to alternate weeks. He was only allowed two visitors at a time and at half-hour intervals, so we thought we could bring other family with us occasionally.

It's impossible to describe in words how it feels to visit your child in jail. I have worked with inmates regularly at the Police Department, picking them up at the jail and taking them to different job sites. I knew the conditions and the turf fighting that went on everyday at the county jail and knowing this only increased my anxiety.

I also knew that Todd, by committing a felony had severely limited his future job opportunities and other endeavors. It was a blemish that he would have to live with the rest of his life.

I was standing in the reception area of the jail and my eyes started to water up like crazy. A deputy entered the room and gave instructions to all of us who were visiting. One of the inmates' mothers must have noticed my tears welling up in my eyes and whispered it will get easier after the first time. I'm sure her intentions were good, but it certainly wasn't the reassurance I was looking for.

We all had to sign in and provide a picture ID. It was a waiting game from that point. Another deputy finally came out and read off twelve names of families in the room. My name wasn't called off. I then discovered that only so many could enter at a time and each one had a half-hour to spend with their family member. It was first come first serve so I learned to get there at least an hour before visiting time.

After what seemed to be a lot longer than a half an hour, the second group of names was called and I was in that group. We were led to a large elevator and the guard called on his radio to have the elevator doors opened. We piled in and the deputy radioed to have the elevator locked down and sent to the second floor visitors' area. We arrived to the second floor the deputy read off several names and about half of the group filed out of the elevator. He directed them to go around the corner and he then radioed again to have the elevator shut.

The rest of the visitors and I were dropped off the elevator on the third floor. I followed the group just around the corner through a thick steel door. The room we entered had six glass windows with stone pillars protruding on each side. In front of each window was a stool and attached to the pillars were direct line phones. Some of the inmates had two visitors and they had to take turns sitting and speaking. On the other side of the glass was a room which was the mirror image of room where we were seated.

Six inmates were soon escorted into the room through a door on the left side of the room. Todd came in second and I can't fully describe the immediate shock I felt at the moment. I didn't want to show Todd my hurt feelings, but I couldn't hold back the tears that welled up in my eyes as I saw him in his orange jumpsuit. His eyes finally made contact with my face and his smile immediately turned into an expression of remorse. He knew he had hurt me and immediately picked up the phone to talk.

He wanted to reassure me that everything was alright. He said, the guards were okay and guys in his cellblock were not violent. He did tell me that for a few days he would have to sleep on a mattress placed on the cement floor. He said it wasn't that bad and one of the inmates was going to be released on Friday, so he would soon have a bed to sleep in. I will admit the Hendricks County Jail was a lot cleaner and brighter than the one in Marion County where I picked up my inmate workers.

Todd went on to tell me about the commissary where he was able to purchase toiletries, snacks, and writing material. His mother and I had already discussed how we were going to help him get the items he needed. We decided to send an initial amount of forty dollars into his commissary account to get his toiletries, pen, paper and some stamps. Belinda and I then agreed to send him additional ten dollars a week for him to use as needed.

I mentioned this earlier on the phone, but decided to reiterate to Todd that Belinda and I hired an attorney to handle his case. We had heard that the county's court appointed attorneys were overburdened and Todd's case probably wouldn't get much attention. We both wanted Todd to get just enough taste of jail to make him not want to go back, but we didn't want him to spend a year or two there and end up with an extensive record. Belinda knew a corporate attorney who recommended an attorney familiar with criminal law.

We interviewed the attorney and according to him, he was the "best attorney in town." He also told us his fee was $5000.00.

Belinda and I decided to retain his services, but not before we talked to Todd. We told him that we were going to do this for him just one time. If he ever messed up again he would be on his own as far as attorneys and commissary money. He thanked us both and promised that he would straighten up, once he got out.

Todd, being off the effects of drugs, was back to his old self again. His main concern was how the rest of the family was taking this, especially my Dad. He even said at one point, he didn't want grandpa to hate him. He told me he wanted to write and apologize to Grandpa and all of his aunts and uncles for his stupid behavior. I told him that grandpa didn't hate him and I encouraged him to write the letters.

After what seemed like a short period of time a guard came down and told us our time was up. Instead of taking the elevator we were allowed to walk the three flights of stairs down to the lobby. I walked directly to my car without turning back and the tears flowed freely most of the thirty-minute trip home.

A few days later I received the following letter from Todd.

Dear Dad,

How are you and Linda doing? I'm doing OK here. I know I call you every week and you visit every other, but I have a few things to tell you that are easier to say by letter.

I want you to know that I am glad you are here to help me through this and without you I wouldn't be able to make it. I need and I'm glad to have you're support.

I have had a lot of time to think and I have learned many things. I guess the first thing I learned is what I did was wrong and I now feel bad for it. I also know, I have a lot of changes to make, but the main reason I wrote this letter was to apologize for the way I treated you.

I know I was wrong in the way I treated you. You brought me into your home and I took advantage of you. We ended on bad terms and that was my fault. I pushed you to the limit and got what I deserved. I treated you as if you had no authority over me and I know I hurt you. I ignored what you said and I shouldn't have. Everything that you said would happen, if I stayed on the same road did. I hope you can forgive me.

I remember growing up we had such good times together and you always stood up for me. We always had fun together and you came to all my games. We watched TV shows together and always sat down to dinner together and even though you whooped my butt in Putt-Putt all the time, I still had fun. But some of the best times we ever had together were when we went on our trips. Such as, California, the Grand Canyon, Las Vegas, Mammoth Cave and etc... It never mattered where we went as long as we were together we had a good time. What I'm really trying to say is, I want my best buddy back.

I wish you and Linda the best and I love you very much.

Your Son,

Todd

P.S. - I would like to join a bowling league with you when I get out.

Todd also enclosed in the envelope a handcrafted certificate. In very large letters he wrote the following.

THE WORLDS GREATEST FATHER AWARD.

This certificate hereby states that on the 18th of June, Mark H. Stahl, the father of Todd Douglas Stahl is named and will always be known as the world's Greatest Father.

On Father's Day Todd wrote and sent me the following poem.

MY DAD

From the day I came home, you were there for me,
No one could have done it better than thee.
You stuck by me through thick and thin,
Even when I lose or when I win.

Growing up in life, I looked up to you,
And if times were rough, you always knew.
You've struggled sometimes, but I always came first,
And when you were angry, never did you curse.

When mom and I were fighting, you took me inside,
And we often made travels, too far and wide.
You kept me in high school till I was done,
And often reminded me that I'm number one

I know I've let you down in many ways,
And with your forgiveness I can start a new day,
I will love you always through good and through bad,
And that's why you should know I call you my dad.

Happy Father's Day and I love you,

Todd

On July 28, 1999 Todd wrote me another letter.

Dad,

I'm glad you came to visit me yesterday, and I'm glad you brought Ryan with you. But maybe next time you can come by yourself. Not that I didn't like talking to Ryan, but I would like to talk to you too.

Well it's almost time to go to court. I really cannot wait. I hope that Eric (his attorney) works something out with the prosecutor so that I can come home soon. You are looking pretty good now days. I guess Linda must be taking care of you. I really am going to miss living with you, but I figure it's for the best. Not being over around Beech Grove all the time will definitely keep me out of trouble. I would still like to come over and visit a lot.

As for me I've had almost 3 months to think about what has been going on. I truly believe I am a changed person. I don't feel the same way about things as I did before. I have also found out that besides God family is the most important thing in my life. I am still reading this career book trying to decide what I want to study when I go to school

I received a letter from Grandpa today and he told me about how he and grandma were making tomato sauce. I plan to write him tonight also. I cannot wait to see grandma and grandpa again. Anyway only 2 weeks from tomorrow I go to court. I cannot wait. In the meantime I'm just going to let time pass while I keep busy. I miss you very much.

Tell Linda I said hi. I hope she knows I care for her too. I am glad she is there for you, but also for me. Let her know she is a very nice lady, and I can think of nobody else as good for you. I love you both.

Your Son,

Todd

Todd wrote similar letters to his grandparents, aunts, and uncle's. The following are a couple of letters he wrote to my mom and dad.

Dear Grandma and Grandpa,

How are you doing? I'm sorry I had to write you like this. I know you must be upset and likewise you should be. I've let you down and caused you pain and suffering. I hope you will still be there for me when I get out. I love you very much and want you to forgive me. I know what I've done is wrong and there is nothing I can do to make up for it. But being in here I have realized something, and when I get out I'm going to change. You really don't understand what you have until something like this happens. You've been there all my life for me and I messed up. This letter is very hard for me to write because of these circumstances. Everyday I hope and pray that you will be there for me when I get out. I hung around the wrong crowd and ended up exactly how my dad said I would. I treated everyone badly and I have a lot of things to take care of. I'm going to miss a lot of things being in here and I just want to apologize for everything. Please understand that this hurts me very much and I will never forget what you've done for me. I love you.

Todd

PS. I did one other stupid thing and got a tattoo.

June 1, 1999

Dear Grandpa and Grandma,

Thank you for sending that birthday card. It makes me feel good to know you haven't given up on me. Somehow I knew you would still be there for me and that is what is most important to me.

You are right about starting over that's what I plan to do. With the changes and the increase in faith I'm going to make, I know I will better my self as a person.

Today Ryan and my dad came to see me. I have realized I am missing a lot and have much to do when I get out. The love I have established for my parents and family will be shown when this is all over. Life is full of its ups and downs and this is one of those downs.

Yesterday I watched the Bulls beat the Pacers. Even though the Pacers played tough. Jordan was too much for them. I finished reading my first book and look forward to start the new book my dad brought me today. They still haven't taken us outside and I wish they would. I miss you both very much and look forward to seeing you. I keep you in my heart and mind, and love you always. As the days go by I must always keep my head up.

Todd

PS. You may write back if you wish it would be greatly appreciated.

I felt it necessary to include all these letters for I believe it shows the Todd I knew best. The loving, caring Todd that wasn't on drugs. I really believe Todd was very sincere with every letter he wrote. He hated being in jail and he couldn't wait to get out and start over. He also knew he hurt the ones he loved the most and the ones he could count on to love him too.

Todd spent four months in jail; he missed his nineteenth birthday in May and the whole summer. In September, Todd's case finally went to court. Belinda, my sister Clare, and I drove to Danville for the trial. Clare hadn't seen Todd in his orange jail uniform before and nearly went into tears. I had seen handcuffed prisoners escorted in an out of the Marion county jail many times, but nothing can prepare you for the shock of seeing your own child in shackles attached to and paraded in a courtroom with several other prisoners.

Eric told Todd to plead guilty when the judge asks him. The judge then gave Todd a stern lecture, four month in jail (the time he already served), and two years of probation. Todd's attorney told us after the trial that if he stayed out of trouble during his probation period his record would be expunged.

Todd was really excited to be getting out of jail that day and his mother, Clare, and I went to the jail and waited for his release. We stopped on the way back home at a pizza place where Todd was delighted to have something other than the jail food he had been eating.

Belinda had agreed to allow Todd to move back into her house, with some ground rules established. The first above all the rest was he'd have to get a job immediately and pay rent as soon as he could. Todd agreed to all of her terms and he soon found employment building fences with the company that employed his cousin Ryan.

The next three months were great. Todd asked me if I wanted to be his partner on a two-person winter bowling league team and I enthusiastically agreed. We had a great time at the neighborhood bowling alley every Tuesday night. I would pick him up early and sometimes we would go to dinner first. Todd was an excellent bowler with an average in the high 170s. He had won several youth league tournaments and won some scholarship money, which he never used.

Todd and Ryan's boss was also the owner of the fencing company that employed them. He just happened to be a guy

I went to high school with and grew up close to where Ryan's mother lived. Eventually word got back to me that both boys were doing a great job. Todd was back to being himself and things couldn't have been going better. Unfortunately those days were short lived and some of his bad patterns started to resurface.

CHAPTER 11

It was the morning of day nine and a nurse walked into the waiting room to inform us that Todd had a very rough night. She didn't tell me anything I didn't know already. I had walked back to Todd's room several times during the night and watched the monitor fluctuate up and down.

Linda and I had gone home long enough to shower and change clothes. I can remember telling Linda that we needed to get back to the hospital right away. I had finally realized that Todd was going to die and I sincerely felt this was his last day.

I don't know exactly what time the hospital staff came to get us, but it seemed to be early evening. They told us that the medication wasn't able to control Todd's brain from swelling. The nurse said they were going to discontinue his treatment and test for brain activity.

I don't remember why but it was supposed to take six hours to complete the test. Belinda and I began to call family members. Later that night the staff allowed us all to go back into Todd's room to wait. Belinda, Brandi, Linda, and I positioned ourselves around Todd's bed. Sitting on the floor behind us stood and sat several of our family members. The long night's vigil began.

Belinda was holding Todd's hand and stroking it gently. Brandi was on the other side of Todd gently sliding her hand along his arm. I sat on a stool nearby and Linda was sitting on the floor next to me.

All of our eyes were fixed on the brain pressure monitor next to Todd's bed, the digital reading was up to twenty-eight. After twenty minutes the monitor's reading slowly crept past thirty and nearly everyone broke down in tears. It was only the beginning of the longest and worst night of my life. It was the night I watched my son die.

There was a clock on the wall that seemed to move in slow motion. I couldn't help but remember the phone call I received from Belinda the previous November following Todd's release from jail. She told me she was having problems with Todd again and would have to kick him out of the house if he didn't straighten up. I asked to speak to Todd and she handed him the phone.

Todd immediately went into one of his old tirades about how his mother wanted to dictate to him how to conduct his affairs. I asked him what the problem was and he said she was trying to tell him whom he could hang out with. It was then I found out he had hooked up with some of his old gang members and he was out late every night. Todd said, Belinda had placed a curfew on him and he was supposed to be home every work night at ten o'clock. I told him that he was living in his mother's house and he needed to abide by her rules. He said that he was nineteen years old and didn't need us to tell him who his friends could be and what time he should be in at night. He also said he was leaving again and knew a place where he could live and he hung up.

I talked to Belinda later that night and she said he stormed off. She also told me she was having a heck of a time getting him up each morning and she didn't believe he was going to work. It sounded as if Todd was using drugs again.

Todd didn't return to Belinda's home that night, but came back the next day to pick up his belongings. He called me and said he was moving to Martinsville, a town about twenty-five miles south of Indy. He told me he wouldn't be able to bowl with me anymore. He said, he didn't have a ride to town.

I didn't want to completely lose contact with him, so I told him I'd pick him up. I wanted to keep the lines of communication open so I could maybe talk some sense into him.

For the next five months, I picked Todd up every week, in a remote area near Martinsville. He was living with a friend's family that he had known from our old apartment complex. I didn't know what the living arrangements were, but I knew Todd wasn't working. Todd would say they were friends who were just letting him stay there.

It was a thirty-five minute drive to Martinsville. Todd would always meet me by the road even in the worst part of winter. Todd had definitely changed once again. He was quiet, although more argumentative when he did speak. On several occasions he told me he didn't care if I picked him up to go bowling anymore, but he never closed the door completely. About three quarters into the season he said he couldn't pay for his bowling so I offered to pay his way and I would take it out of his prize money at the end of the year. He said I didn't have to do that and we could just quit. I reminded him of my rule about finishing what we started in order to give him a reason not to quit. The real reason was that I wanted to show him I was still there if he needed to talk.

Bowling nights were not the only time I saw Todd. I took him to Danville every month to visit his probation officer. Periodically they would test him for drugs and for awhile he was all right. In February of that winter he was tested again and the following month he was told his test came back cloudy and he was tested again. He was told at the time if the test came back bad again he would have to go back to jail.

Todd was really hot when he came out of the office. He ranted and raved about how the test wasn't right. I told him I guess we'll find out when he goes back next month if it was right or not. He said it wasn't fair and this means that if he messes up again he'll have this strike against him already. I told him simply don't mess up again and life isn't always fair.

The next month Todd's drug test came back negative and he was really relieved. I believe that threat of going back to jail and the fact that his friend's family was moving to Pennsylvania was a wake up call for Todd.

On the way to the bowling alley in late March, Todd told me he was talking to a neighbor about getting a job roofing houses. In April, the family he was staying with did move back to their home state, with the exception of the son that was Todd's age. Todd then started working again and in June he and his friend rented an apartment together in Martinsville. Todd was back to his normal self once again. He was friendly, excited about his job, and must have been doing fairly well at it. I'd pick him at the job site to take him to the probation office and he looked like he really knew what he was doing.

Todd was finally fulfilling some of his other court ordered duties too. He started a twelve-step program and performed community service work in the Martinsville area. He also started dating Brandi, a Martinsville high school senior, for whom he really fell head over heels. I had mixed emotions about the relationship; Todd told me the twelve-step program warned him against dating at this stage. Todd's attitude appeared so great that I guess I didn't see the harm.

Brandi seemed to have been the best thing that happened to Todd in a long time. She had a little boy and Todd became very close to him and for nearly a year everything was great. I can remember Todd going out and buying everyone Christmas presents with his own money and really feeling good about it. While taking Todd to Brandi's house, quite often he'd ask me to stop someplace so he could buy her some flowers.

There was a winter dance at the high school and Todd couldn't wait to go. He showed me the picture of him and Brandi at the dance and he looked so happy.

He even said he was encouraging Brandi to do better in school so she could graduate, which I thought was ironic since I had such a hard time getting Todd to do the same thing.

It had been a long time since I'd seen him so happy; unfortunately his happiness wouldn't last.

CHAPTER 12

I looked at Brandi standing near Todd's hospital bed and I thought how nice it was that he had known that special kind of love. Todd's brain pressure monitor slowly crept past fifty and everyone broke down once again in tears. It must have been around midnight when Ryan, his dad and mom came by and said they were leaving. Brandi's ride couldn't wait any longer and she too had to leave. She said, she'd be back to visit tomorrow. It didn't register to Belinda, Linda, and I until after she left that perhaps she didn't realize Todd wouldn't be here in the morning.

We thought about calling her, but we decided to wait until morning. I didn't know much about Brandi other than what Todd told me. Apparently she had experienced problems in inner city Indianapolis where she grew up and her parents decided it best to move out to the country. I can say from what little contact I had with her; she seemed to be a very pleasant young lady. It's unfortunate that Todd's next run in with trouble may have stemmed from his relation with her.

Todd's behavior was starting to get erratic again soon after the first of the year. His roommate Brian had decided to follow his girlfriend down to Florida where her family had relocated. I went to visit Todd one Sunday and we were supposed to go out to lunch. When I picked him up he looked like he had been beaten to a pulp. Around both of his eyes were huge black and blue circles and red lacerations were scattered across his face and head.

He said one of his friends from his old gang came down to visit and they got into a fight. His story of what happened changed each time he told it. He first blamed it completely on his friend and then on both of them being drunk and acting crazy.

I think I was able to fill in the blanks enough to figure what had happened. I had heard from my nephew once that Todd was a mean drunk. He started talking trash and thought he could whip everyone. I tend to believe that was what happened the night before I came to visit. He and his friend got into it and Todd got the worst of it.

In the next couple of months I noticed Todd getting worse. He started lying again and acting nervous. Once he showed up at the house in a car, which he said a friend had loaned him. I told him his license was suspended and he wasn't supposed to be driving at all. He of course made up some lame excuse about needing to come up to Indy to meet someone, but I knew something was up. I had never seen him this nervous before to the point where his hands were shaking. I took him to dinner at a fast food restaurant and he told me he was going over to visit Grandpa too. He said, he wanted to get some can food from him for a picnic he was going to with Brandi. My Dad always had an abundance of can goods and would let the three grandkids go shopping in his basement cupboards.

I wasn't buying Todd's story and I knew that by the way he was acting it would certainly scare my Dad. I took him to the grocery store and allowed him to pick up a few things, which I paid for and sent him on his way. I later found out he still went over to Dad's and picked up some more stuff. I'm sure he also hit his Grandpa up for some cash too. He had this way about telling

Dad he didn't have any money for something and my dad would always come through.

A month later I finally got fed up with his antics and told him he needed to straighten up. I asked him how Brandi put up with him and he finally confessed that Brandi had broken up with him a while back. He also said nothing matters anyway, because there was a warrant out for his arrest. He said his last urine test came back positive for crack cocaine. He said he had already told his mother. I called Belinda and together we convinced him to turn himself in.

I drove down to Martinsville on a Saturday in early May and rented a truck. Todd and I put all of his stuff into storage and I dropped him off at his moms. Todd said weekends were bad at the jail, because all the drunks were being processed and decided it would be best to wait until Monday to turn himself in. Todd and his mother went to church together on Sunday and on that Monday she delivered him to the Hendricks County Jail. The day before was mother's day.

Todd's second stay at the Hendricks County Jail was different than the first. His mother and I kept our word and didn't send him any spending money. Todd said, he didn't expect us to and he knew he put himself there. We did pitch in money, just enough to buy some toiletries. He would also have to make do with a court appointed attorney. We still took turns visiting him every week and I let him call me once a week.

Todd's attitude was different too. He seemed to be a little more hardened this time. It was like he knew the ropes and it didn't bother him to be there. Oh don't get me wrong, he wanted out bad, but he wasn't as apprehensive.

The third week Todd was in jail it was my week to visit. I could tell he was upset and I asked him what was wrong. He said he got into a fight and they may charge him with assault. I asked if he started it and he said, "No, one of my buddies did. I just jumped in to help."

Todd's had spent another birthday in jail too. He had now spent his nineteenth and twenty-first birthdays in jail. I dropped off a card and a book for him to read. He called me that night to thank me. Todd also wrote the following letters while he was in jail a second time.

Dad,

How's it going? Everything's the same here, it always is. I'm just sitting here trying to decide what to do. I was thinking about going outside for a walk. (Just kidding.) Its not that bad in here, but I would much rather be out. I almost forgot how boring this place is.

I'm doing ok, I finally received a mat today to sleep on, and next week I have a bunk. My lawyer/public defender still hasn't contacted me so I can't talk to him about moving my court date up. The correction officers here don't do anything. If you ask them to get you something they say they will, but they don't.

Dad you know I did not want this to happen. I don't like being here. I know what I must put you through and, I am sorry. If I could do it over and change it I would. I'm not a criminal anymore. I was an addict going through a tough time. I couldn't help it when Brandi and I spilt up; I was depressed, and didn't think straight. That is the only reason I'm in here.

The letter you wrote me before I come here was nice. I know you will never give up on me, and that is good to have family that cares about me that much. But I'm not really depressed because I'm in jail it's Brandi, I know there's more girls out there, but I can't get over her. It's like I'm alone without her. Every time

I think about her I get sad. Dad I miss her. Well that's enough about her. What have you been doing? How's Linda?

I miss you dad. I know your there for me just like you always have been. I hope Grandpa, Aunts Clare, Jackie and everyone aren't mad at me. Tell Linda I said hi and everyone else too.

I still don't know what I'm gonna do when I get out. I don't know where I will stay, but I will figure it out.

That's all for now. Please keep me in touch and let me know if you find out anything.

Your Son,

Todd

On June 16, 2000, Todd wrote the following letter where he was worried about the fight he and another inmate got into.

Dad,

How are you doing? I'm still worried about this recent incident. They still won't tell me what they are going to do. I wish I could go back, I would have never done anything, and wouldn't have let my anger get the best of me. It's too late now and I'm worried they will fry me.

That is not why I'm writing this letter. I'm writing this to wish you a Happy Father's Day. I know this isn't exactly where I should be wishing it from, but it's the best I can do for now. You have always been there for me and you are the best dad a son could have. I miss you very much, and I hope we can do things together again soon. I know I have disappointed you on many occasions and I'm sorry I just want to get out of here and start my life over. I know I have you and you will always be there for me and I am fortunate to have someone like you as a father. I look up to you and your relationship with Linda and hope that one day I will find someone that cares for me like that. You are an inspiration to me and I love you.

That's basically all that I want to write you for. I miss you and hope to see you next week at visitation, if not it is ok. I will call you on Sunday.

Happy Fathers Day

Love Your Son (and Best Buddy)

Todd

Once again I didn't doubt Todd's sincerity when he wrote those letters, but I will admit I was wondering if he'd be able to control his behavior after he got out. I knew that whatever Todd did, I could forgive him, but it would take time for me to trust him.

I don't know exactly when Brandi and Todd got back together, but I know it started when she answered a letter he wrote her while he was in jail. I also know that Todd didn't believe there was a problem with his drinking alcoholic beverages. He probably thought that since it was legal it was okay for him to drink. Of course getting behind the wheel of a car after drinking is not only illegal, it's downright stupid.

I don't believe Todd ever really thought things out. Todd may have thought he had a drug addiction problem, but never really recognized he had other addiction problems too. I know a little about being addicted to something, after all I smoked cigarettes for eighteen years. I was up to three packs a day until Todd came home from preschool that day and begged me to quit. I knew smoking wasn't good for me, but I just didn't have enough incentive to quit.

It was sometime in June when Todd first met with his court appointed attorney. The attorney basically said he'd looked into the case. By the middle of July Todd found out he could bail himself out after a certain period of time. It wasn't long after that Todd started working on his mother and me about loaning him the money.

Todd owed the apartment complex where he lived about six months back rent and made arrangements to pay it off a little at a time. He owed Belinda some money too and she was willing to bail him out under certain conditions. He agreed and just two weeks before the accident he was released from jail.

He had started working at his uncle's excavation company the week after he got out. John, Belinda's brother-in-law, told me at the hospital that Todd had been an exceptional worker and he was glad he had hired him. He said it was getting harder and harder to find good workers.

I saw Todd on Monday, just two days before the accident. We went over to my dad's house where Todd cut his grass for him. The three of us had dinner at the Big Boy Restaurant, which was the last time we talked face to face. He seemed real happy with his job and he had plans to make things right in his life. He even talked about going back to school. My son was back again.

CHAPTER 13

The brain pressure monitor had now slowly crept to seventy-five; none of us had expected the monitor would reach that high. I had fallen asleep and fell off the stool I was sitting on several times due to the total exhaustion of the past several days. I could feel Linda's hand gently stroking my leg as she sat below me on the floor. I noticed several times during the night Linda and Belinda's head would rise and fall trying to fight off sleep. My sister and many of Belinda's family members still lined the hallway behind us.

It was around five in the morning and the brain pressure monitor reached eighty and then it rapidly took off one click at a time. It passed one hundred and we all broke down again and it kept on going. When it reached one hundred and twenty it stopped its forward progression and started to reverse itself. The digital read out finally rested to a stop at eighty-five and we knew it was over.

A nurse came in and told us another test had to be run and the results wouldn't be available for several hours. We all got up and slowly left his room. I can remember being totally drained physically and mentally. I looked at Linda, my sister, and Belinda's brother and said I needed to lie down. They led me to a private waiting room I laid down on a couch and quickly succumbed to my exhaustion.

I don't know how long I was out, but I figured it was around two or three hours. I remember hearing voices out in the hall and I slowly rolled off the couch. Linda was in the room sitting in a chair across from where I had been sleeping. She said that they were waiting for me to wake up so we could discuss some things together.

My sister Clare, Belinda, and several of her relatives were in the hallway, when Belinda approached me. She said that we needed to meet with Father Wilmoth now that I was up. We went back into the private waiting room and the priest counseled us on how to proceed. He said, we could call him later to finalize the funeral arrangements, but asked if we considered asking for donations at Todd's viewing. He threw out several options, but none seemed to strike me appropriate. Belinda asked me what I thought and several charities popped into my mind. I named a couple and then I thought of MADD, Mothers Against Drunk Driving. Belinda thought that was a great idea and we agreed it was the organization we wanted to support.

After meeting with Father Wilmoth, Belinda told me that there were representatives from the organ donor program who wanted to speak with us. A young man and women stepped into the room and we were asked if we would listen to information on their program.

I must interject at this time to explain the emotions I and all of the family were feeling at this time. We were all grasping for answers and wanting to make sense of why Todd had to die so young. We were literally reaching out to make things right. Maybe by his death several other people would benefit, either through donations to MADD or an organ transplant so someone else may live.

I won't even try to remember the man's name that spoke with us about the organ donor program. I was acting almost mechanically by this point, since I was totally fatigued mentally. He introduced his companion and said she was in training and would we mind if she sat in. We both nodded in agreement.

The man began by offering his sincere condolences for our loss. He seemed to be sincere, yet I couldn't help but think how routinely he must deliver that message. He went on to rattle off statistics on how many lives are saved each year through the program. He even gave specific examples on how some people had benefited over the years.

He went on to tell us he couldn't guarantee any successful results by allowing them to harvest Todd's organs, but could only cite examples how it has helped so many others. The man didn't pressure us at all and even left the room with his associate while Belinda and I discussed what we wanted to do.

Belinda and I agreed to donate some of Todd's organs. The gentleman and the lady returned and we started the process. We were asked about Todd's medical background and we provided him Todd's medical history. The gentleman then asked about our medical history at this time we told the man Todd was adopted and we had no medical records for the biological parents. He then asked about Todd's lifestyle and we could only answer a few of his questions.

Did Todd do drugs? Yes, we both said in unison. Was Todd HIV positive? We couldn't answer. What did we know of Todd's sexual behavior? We couldn't answer. Did Todd drink alcohol? We both nodded yes. Did we know if Todd shared needles? We couldn't answer that question either.

They then proceeded to ask us what body parts they could "harvest" and, yes, they used the term harvest. First they asked about the internal organs such as, the liver, heart, and lungs. We both agreed to those organs being used. It was when they got to the external parts of the body; I started to feel uncomfortable. When he asked about his skin, I revolted and said no! I just couldn't imagine them stripping pieces of skin from his body. I don't know why, here I felt okay with them wrenching his guts out; I just couldn't stand the thought of them removing the skin. They asked about his eyes too, but I can't even remember what I said to those.

When the questions were all answered the lady who had been writing things down on a clipboard handed it to Belinda and I to read and sign. We both signed the paper and I recall that my hand was shaking the whole time.

We all left the waiting room and found that none of our family members had left.

We stood in the hall of the hospital for a short while and a nurse came over to talk with Belinda who was standing with her sisters and brothers. Belinda and the nurse walked over to Linda, Clare, and I and told us what the nurse had said. The last test results were in and Todd was legally declared dead. I broke down and cried out "Is it all over," and she nodded. I asked if we could see him one last time and the nurse said yes.

I can remember Belinda and me not walking, but running back to Todd's bedside. I threw myself across his body shouting to take comfort in the Lord, to seek out his grandmother, (Belinda's mother had died of cancer several years before), my grandparents, a childhood friend who had passed away in the fourth grade. I just didn't want him to be alone.

We finally tore ourselves away from his bed and started to leave the hospital. As we walked through the tunnel leading to the garage. I broke down again and Belinda's brother Don placed his hand on my shoulder.

I can't tell you much about the rest of that day. I didn't feel like talking to anyone, so my wife fielded most of the phone calls. I did speak to Todd's mother about some of the arrangements that had to be made.

I woke up the next morning in a deep depression. I kept thinking about the next few days, meeting with the funeral director and then the viewing and funeral itself. I was wondering how I was going to get through it all.

Then it hit me. Where was Todd? I had prayed every day of Todd's life that he would some day acknowledge the Lord. Repeatedly over the years Todd had been taught the formula of salvation. Even as he lay unconscious in the hospital, I once leaned close to his ear and whispered "Accept the Lord," but I had no way of knowing if he even heard me.

Any parent could imagine what I must have been feeling. I may not ever see my only child again. My grief was so overwhelming I didn't know how I was going to continue on. It was at this lowest point of my life that I cried out, "Lord Please Help Me!"

It's hard to describe what happen to me the moment I uttered those words. It was as if the cloud of my despair had been pushed out of my body. I don't know how many of you have experienced the Holy Spirit, but this was like He was there removing my doubt and fear.

I don't know exactly when Todd acknowledged the Lord. It may have been prior to the accident or while he lay by the side of the road, it didn't matter. I knew my son had made that choice. I know some of you may not believe this part of the story, some our wondering how I can I be so sure of my son's salvation. Well to tell you the truth it doesn't matter what anyone else believes, because that miracle of acknowledgement was for me and the answer to my prayer. My son was going to be alright.

The Holy Spirit left me with a message that day and I immediately placed it on paper. That message was read at my son's funeral.

Before I read those words to you, let me tell you how my son's death has affected my life. Yes, the Lord provided me the strength to continue but there hasn't been a day gone by that I haven't missed my son.

I can remember the day after Todd's passing I asked my wife to take down and hide all of his pictures. Three months later I asked her to replace them. Six months had gone by before I could muster the courage to visit Todd's grave site. I now go several times a year but never without shedding a tear.

My wife and I decided to get away for a week just two months after Todd's accident. We went to a place where Todd and I had visited six years earlier. My eyes would fill with tears each time we passed the miniature golf course that Todd and I frequented as I was reminded of his laughter.

The vacation was nice overall and I felt slightly refreshed. When we arrived home, I picked up the stack of mail and started sorting through it. When I saw one from the Organ Donor program I immediate opened and read it. In essence this is what it said. It started by offering once again their condolences, and also thanked us for donating Todd's organs. We regret to inform you that your son's heart, lungs, etc were not in suitable condition for transplant. We determined your son's liver as healthy and was transplanted into a nineteen year old girl. Regretfully, she died of complications while in recovery. I threw the letter down and went to my room in tears, asking myself when will it all end?

To this day I haven't visited the restaurant my father, Todd, and I dined at just two days before his accident. Todd's birthday and of course the day he died are still not good days. Todd and I would always look forward to all the holidays. Now I spend part of each of those days at the cemetery placing flowers upon my son's grave.

Up in the attic of my home are all of Todd's toys including his GI Joes, I rarely go up there. When I was younger I collected over two thousand comic books that I was going to give to Todd. They are sitting on the floor of a closet and on top of that closet is a cardboard container with all of Todd's drawings, school work, and father day cards. This box from it's inception we had both simply called, "Todd's box."

Today I am now a member of a relatively small group of parents who have out lived their children. New friends and old acquaintances sometimes ask do you have any children. I normally say, yes, but he's passed away. The reaction I get is first condolences and then kind of a backing off of any conversation

I love the memories I have of Todd, and when someone will tell me a story about their children I would happily relate one of Todd's. Unfortunately, people can't relate to my feelings and become uncomfortable when I talk about him. Parent's talking about their children never bothers me, but I have to admit being a little envious of those who talk about their grand children. I was really looking forward to be a doting grandfather some day.

Now I would like to share with you some lessons I have learned from my experience as a father. A parent needs to take an active part of their children's life. If you truly love them do what ever you can to keep them on the right path.

Children, I have read you the letter Todd wrote to me while in jail. He tells how he wished he had listened to me. No one cares about you or loves you more than your parents. Think about it, what ulterior motive could your parents have? They only want the best for you. So when they tell you something. Please listen.

Don't do drugs. Don't start and if you are already under the influence seek help immediately. Drinking too much alcohol is also dangerous and drinking and driving is just plain stupid. There is a mentality that doing drugs and drinking isn't hurting anyone but those who are doing it. After hearing my story I hope you realize that isn't the case. I miss my son dearly.

On September 9, 2002, exactly two years since Todd's passing I finished the first draft of this my story. This is what I wrote on that day.

Yesterday Linda and I placed flowers on Todd's grave. Today I went back alone to the cemetery and spent time talking to my best buddy. Then with tears flowing I slowly walked away.

Now I would I'd like to share some thoughts with all of you who have faith in God. As a parent I have learned a great deal about man's relationship with the Creator. I loved Todd with all my heart. Yes, I would get angry and even disappointed with him, but I could never turn my back on him. God feels the same way about His children. Remember that the Lord loves us all and is with us in every step we take. If you put complete faith and trust in the Lord, you will be able to rely on Him in every circumstance that comes your way.

Now for the Spirit driven message that was read at my son's funeral, which I have titled. "A PARENTS LOVE"

A PARENTS LOVE

(Todd's Eulogy)

I want to offer a heart felt thanks to each and every one of you for your support during this time. I don't have to tell you how much this tragedy has grieved me.

Any parent knows that losing a child is the worst thing that could ever happen to them. I've been going through numerous emotions: some of which many of you have probably experienced as well.

We tend to "what if" or blame ourselves repeatedly. We wish we could have done something different in Todd's life that could have changed the outcome of the night of his accident. However, what we need to concentrate on is our fondest wish, which is that Todd's short life not be in vain. Those of you who have had the privilege of knowing my son may choose to draw upon you own memories. I hope you will cherish his memory, but further, I hope you will share those memories and the lessons you have learned with people you meet along life's journey.

I would like to take a moment to share with you some of my memories of my life with Todd.

When Todd was only five years old, I was holding a friend's two-year old son at a sporting event. The child and I were interacting playfully and Todd was sitting a few seats down with another friend. I watched Todd as he kept looking jealously back at me. Before long he was sitting right beside me vying for my attention.

It was at that time that I explained to Todd that he was my best buddy...he always had been and always would be. I went on to explain that I would always love him no matter what.

When Todd was in the third grade I picked him up from his mother's house, and I could tell he was very nervous. Water started to swell up in his eyes and I asked him what was wrong. He burst into tears and told me he had gotten into trouble at school that day. I can't remember the offense, but I told him he was grounded for a week. He burst into tears again and said, " Oh good, I thought you'd hate me and never want to pick me up again." I was stunned by his response. I explained to him that as a parent I had to punish him, but he must always remember that no matter what, I would always love him.

In his late teens and even until recently Todd had gone through some rough times. He made some bad choices, choices his mother and I could not support. He accused us at times of not understanding and not loving him. We both tried to convince him that even though we could not agree with his line of thinking, or the choices he made, we would always love him, no matter what.

I am very fortunate to have a strong faith in the Lord. I can't mention all the things He has done for me in such a short period of time, but I find it necessary to share a few. The first is that He allowed me the gift of being Todd's father. Secondly, He consoles me. As Todd lay in the hospital for over a week struggling for life, I felt so helpless. I had no control over what was going on, and realizing this, I had to leave it in God's hands. His will may not be the same as mine, but I choose to believe the Lord knew the full extent of Todd's injuries and, therefore, took him into His loving arms so he would not have to suffer anymore.

That brings me to the next gift the Lord has given me, and that is the affirmation that Todd is in a very wonderful and glorious place now. I will see and be with "my best buddy" again.

Finally, I would like to thank the Lord for being who He is. God is all things. He is our creator, and we are His children. I know that as Todd lay in that hospital bed, he felt the presence of all his family. He knew we all loved him, and I know he now understands that his mother and I will always love him, no matter what.

Parents who are here... please take this time to reflect upon your children and tell them how much you love them. Children... please understand that your parents' love is unconditional. And to all of you, please remember that like a parent, we have a Heavenly Father who will always love us, no matter what.

www.ingramcontent.com/pod-product-compliance
Lightning Source LLC
LaVergne TN
LVHW050555160826
845677LV00011B/2323

* 9 7 9 8 3 5 3 6 6 2 6 5 5 *